Inspiring You to Kickstart Your Success Journey

THE TAO OF A MASTER Connector

The "way" an introvert became a Master Connector

STEVE SPIRO

ISBN: 979-8-218-21379-4

Table of Contents

Foreword

It has been an absolute pleasure to help Steve Spiro take his vision for this book and make it a reality!

Each story shared here is a "nugget of gold" that inspires, motivates, encourages, or empowers you to be better, to do better, and to try!

As Steve said, "I love the idea of being the light. I believe it's our mission on this planet to be the light. If we can help shine a light, lift up other people, and add value to people, what a great world this would be."

Throughout this book, Steve talks a lot about uplifting others and being of service to them. I'm all for that, and one of the reasons why I believe in his mission is to find ways to make this world a better place.

"A candle loses nothing by lighting another candle."
~James Keller

Steve is exceptional at sharing his light with others and helping them find their inner greatness so that they can shine their light too.

Thank you, Steve, for allowing me the privilege of helping you bring your dream to life! This book is amazing – and so are you!

Val Roskens Tews

People don't always need advice. Sometimes all they need is a hand to hold, an ear to listen, and a heart to understand them.

MASTER connector tip

#MasterConnector

Introduction

My Life Story

My Beginning

I was born and raised in the Bronx. My parents did not have a lot of money and struggled financially. When I was 11 years old, they got divorced. As a single parent, my mom went back to college. She wanted a career that would allow her to provide a decent life for us. We still struggled, but it was okay because it was all part of the journey.

Growing up, I was bullied and picked on. I was learning disabled and dyslexic, which I didn't realize at the time. I knew I had some reading challenges. When asked to speak in class, I would turn beet red and stutter. It was horrible!

My parents put me in a Judo class for a few months. Unfortunately, it made things worse for me with the kids in the neighborhood. Once they found out I was taking Judo, they'd tease me, saying, "Hey, let's see what kind of skills you got!" And then they picked on me even more!

It wasn't a good experience, but it did leave an impression in my brain. I remember my Judo uniform and how it smelled. Something about it was intriguing to me. I think this contributed to my desire to learn martial arts later in my life when I was 20 years old.

My dad owned a liquor store in New York City, and I was dissuaded from going into that industry. Instead, I attended the High School of Art and Design and majored in graphic design and advertising, where I met my wife, Liz. I went to college for advertising as well. When I couldn't find a job after graduating from college, I started my own advertising agency in New York City. It was wild being a 23-year-old businessman.

Parallel to owning my own business, I started training in the martial arts in 1983. I went on to earn a 4th-degree black belt in Goju Ryu karate and a 1st-degree black belt in traditional Japanese Jujitsu. My wife also holds a black belt, which makes our household fun, since both of us are black belts.

Lessons learned

You will read about many of the lessons that I have learned in life in this book. Some came from my martial arts experience, which shaped me because it allowed me to prove to myself that I could work hard. I started to outwork most people around me and passed almost everyone in my class in terms of my rank because I was consistent and worked harder. I stayed committed by following the Sensei's instructions.

I didn't let adversity get in my way and stop me!

As I got older, I found ways to block myself from the hurt I experienced when I was younger and the people who caused that hurt. I stayed busy with my career, martial arts, and other endeavors. I wore my busyness like a "badge of honor." But it also gave me a place to hide and avoid connecting with people. That went on for many years.

Mentoring: amazing, incredible, life-changing

I had a successful advertising career. Once, on a plane to Ireland to work on our Guinness beer account, a co-worker told me about a good friend of his. After the trip, my co-worker introduced me to his friend, who took me under his wing and became a mentor to me. This amazing, incredible experience has definitely been life-changing!

Having a mentor was a huge missing piece in my life!

That mentoring relationship put me on the path to self-development. I started reading more books and listening to audiobooks, and networking started to change my perspective and get me out of my shell. I didn't like speaking to people or conversing with them – all of that was very difficult for me. I was not a people person! Mentoring helped get me out of that dark place.

My mentor helped me change my perspective from inward-focused to being others focused.

As an example of my lack of people skills: One day, my partner in the advertising company said, "I've got great news. The company is sending you to a Dale Carnegie course." It was his way of saying, "Hey – your people skills suck!" It was a great course. A lot of what I learned in that course and from reading "How to Win Friends and Influence People" by Dale Carnegie manifested later in my life. It took some time to sink in, but eventually, it did.

I read that book at least once a year for many years. Sometimes my mentor would ask me, "Have you ever read How to Win Friends and Influence People?" I would answer, "Yeah, I've read it through many times." He would respond with, "You might want to read it again."

Long story short… I continued to grow my people skills and my networking skills. In 2008, I joined LinkedIn and built a profile there.

I started networking after my mentor challenged me: "Why don't you meet three strangers every day?"

That became an endeavor for me to do. There were some fun and some embarrassing moments as I learned to network, but I cultivated and developed my skills significantly. I'm really proud I've been able to do that.

I've also been blessed to develop incredible long-term, meaningful relationships with some of the people I have met, whether out and about, living my life, or through social media. I eventually built a very large network.

Making the best of a forced career change

I worked at a very high level in the advertising industry as an Associate Creative Director of a large marketing firm in Greenwich, Connecticut. The week after 9-11-2001, I was laid off. The attacks impacted the economy, and it changed everything. I had to figure out what to do.

Believe it or not, I ended up in copier sales. I figured I could do anything if I could succeed, and I did very well at it. I moved around a bit and eventually transitioned out of that into business automation consulting. That's been a lot of fun. I've helped companies streamline and automate how they communicate and connect with their clients using artificial intelligence.

Creating the "Master Connector" show

Changing careers, along with other projects, has helped me continue to grow. I am now doing some public speaking and co-hosting a LinkedIn Live broadcast. I've had a lot of fun networking, which is how I met my co-host, Cameron Toth. He had been doing a different live broadcast. I was a guest on his show a couple of times, and I was impressed with him. Long story short, we partnered up and created the "Master Connector" (a LinkedIn Live show), which has been a blast! We've had some amazing guests, including a few high-level show biz people, authors, ex-NFL athletes, and former military, to name a few. It's really been a fun journey.

Sharing my mission and my four pillars

I continue to speak to groups. I love inspiring teams of people and really helping them.

**My mission on this planet:
to be the light, to uplift, inspire, and encourage.**

In this book, you'll see the four pillars I speak about.

Pillar One

Having the grit to overcome obstacles.

Pillar Two

Shifting from being inward-focused to more others-focused, paying it forward, and being a "go-giver."

Pillar Three

Connecting authentically. I love leading with my weakness. I've learned through life that there's power when you lead with your weakness.

Pillar Four

Building a community and growing your connections.

My Ultimate goal for this book

Ultimately, I hope this book will bless you, touch your life, and make a difference. It's been a labor of love. It's my life's journey.

It's also my love letter to God because I want to give Him the credit. I want to give Him the honor and glory. I'm just the vessel.

Hopefully, this book will bless you as much as it has blessed me, knowing that I could really touch lives.

Steve Spiro

My WHY

Traveling

Years ago, my wife and I started traveling. We've been to many different places – Hawaii, Europe, the Caribbean, throughout the United States, and South America. One of our passions is to do a lot more traveling. At some point, we want to have the ability, time, and money to decide, "Okay, tomorrow we want to go to New Zealand," and drive to the airport, grab two tickets, and go! Not have to worry about packing because we'd buy what we needed when we arrived.

Family

We love our family and want to have the money to help them and have time to be there for them.

Financial freedom

We never want to stress or worry about money because when you grow up broke, like my family, that's all we ever thought about. It's about choices and absolute freedom. I heard the three freedoms: financial, time, and location. Sounds great, right? Why not?

Homes

We would love to have a few places around the world, not just the home we own in the northeast United States.

Ultimate why

Ultimately for me, the big "why" – my life's mission – is to make an impact on this world, touch lives, and help people. That really, really drives me, and it's what keeps me going. I've heard it said, "What's your dash?" Everyone has a tombstone when they pass that lists two dates: the date they were born and the date they left this earth to go to the next phase of eternity. There's a dash in between those dates. So what's your dash like? Are you making an impact? Are people better off because you're here? That's a huge why for me.

Life Lessons/Success Principles

Introduction by Chris Salem

Grit is a process that leads to the greatest growth in people over time to be and become more that fulfills their purpose. Angela Duckworth, who coined the term, said, "Grit is passion and perseverance for long-term and meaningful goals." It is the ability to be consistent in something you feel passionate about despite the challenges throughout the process.

This kind of passion is about having intention, direction, and commitment. It's not tied to expectations through intense emotions but embraces the process in the now to focus only on things within your control daily while fully letting go of the rest as part of the process. When you have this kind of passion, you can stay committed to what you can control only with tasks that may be difficult or boring.

So what can you control each day? Here are the five things you can control each day to r apply "grit" in your process:

1. Communication
2. Behavior
3. Attitude
4. Emotions
5. Action

Communication

You can control how you communicate with yourself and others. How do you speak to yourself daily? Is it from your inner champion or inner critic?

How you communicate with yourself plays out subconsciously with others in terms of being codependent or interdependent. Codependent communication can be passive, aggressive, or both simultaneously.

First, some passive people tend to say "Yes" to everything and go out of their way to please and enable others. They do this subconsciously to seek validation from others since they did not receive it from their parent(s) while growing up, and it is embedded as a limiting belief at the subconscious level.

Second, some aggressive people are often perfectionists and tend to place unrealistic or high expectations on others and themselves. They become upset and frustrated when these expectations go unfulfilled, which often they do.

Third, they fluctuate between the two, leading to a lack of clarity and frustration over time.

All three do not support the "grit" process and, in fact, work against it. People operate in the past and future from fear and attach themselves to the outcome. Interdependent communication is assertive, and it's specific, clear, and concise, whether it's the sender or receiver. Assertive people see the bigger picture from "grit" and operate in the "Now," where fear is reduced. They are committed to the process and not attached to the outcome.

Behavior

Like communication, codependent behaviors can be passive, aggressive, or both. They can be assertive, which is consistent in terms of energy and demeanor and does not fluctuate as much. Your behavior can either serve you to impact others in a healthy way or work against you. People who adopt "grit" long-term learn over time to see challenges and obstacles as opportunities to grow, not roadblocks.

Attitude

Attitude is always a choice, like communication and behavior. You can see situations happening for or to you. You see challenges or problems as opportunities to learn and expand when happening for you, or you see them as roadblocks blocking your progress as a victim or from excuses when happening to you. People adopting "grit" see situations happening for and not to them.

Emotions

There are two levels of emotions: primary and secondary. Your primary emotion is your initial reaction internally to a situation that triggers fear. It could be anger, disappointment, or shame or feeling happy, joyful, and radiant. People adopting the "grit" process can learn to control their emotions by choosing to respond to any situation rather than react from their secondary emotions. You will either allow your initial or primary emotion to react to their situation that may not serve you or pause with a deep breath or a few by choosing a positive emotion to respond instead. The power of pause, or taking some deep breaths, is a powerful part of the "grit" process. Before responding, you can ask yourself what you can control versus not control in this situation.

Action

Finally, there is action. You always have control over the level of action you can take daily on any important tasks within your control. You can learn as part of the "grit" process through daily discipline and consistency to "do it" regardless of what the inner critic tells you or how uncomfortable it may be at the moment.

Discipline through consistency that makes the "grit" process chug along includes a daily routine of getting up at the same time every day, making your bed, meditating, journaling, working out, taking a cold shower, eating a healthy breakfast, reading, and reviewing your daily intentions.

Practicing these five things within our control through a daily routine, from discipline and consistency, will change the way we think from reacting to fear in the past and future to responding in the moment not tied to expectations but rather intentions with the level of belief in yourself at that time. It's important to note that fear and what we experience in the past and future are tied to limiting beliefs forged during our developmental years. They minimize our communication, behavior, attitude, emotions, decision-making, and ability to take calculated risks and actions. This often gets people caught up in things they cannot control. Some people get caught up trying to control others' communication, behavior, attitude, emotions, and course of action. In addition, they get caught up in the economy, taxes, weather, and other things beyond our control.

Those who adopt "grit" as part of the process learn and apply the principles to shift their thinking from the past and future to the "now" while only focusing on what they can control daily from intentions and whatever belief level they have about themselves at the moment. Despite the fear from limiting beliefs, they shift away from focusing on what they cannot control and tying expectations to outcomes. They trust the process in the "now" and treat every situation as part of the "grit" process like a puzzle. They focus only on the pieces they control now and let go of the rest, allowing the process to play out to what they can control only that leads to the results they seek long term.

Angela Duckworth's research indicates that the ability to stick with things that are most important to you and bounce back from failure is an essential component of success independent of and beyond what talent and intelligence contribute. She said, "*It is a driver of achievement and success, independent of and beyond what talent and intelligence contribute.*"

Grit to accomplish something important long-term is not tied to being naturally smart or having talent. It requires thinking in the moment, trusting the process only to what you can control, and persevering through the process. Without grit, talent, and skill will fall short of unmet potential. Only with effort does talent become a skill that leads to success.

Steve Spiro clearly learned to overcome his limiting beliefs and not allow them to define him to accomplish great things in his life as a "Master Connector" and chose to be a prime example for others to do for themselves. In his book, you will see that we are all human beings that have struggles and setbacks. It's always your choice to limit yourself or rise above through "grit" to be your best while being an example for others to do the same.

—Chris Salem

You Have to See It to Achieve It

I know the cliché is: you have to see it to *believe* it – but I'm saying you've got to see it to *achieve* it. I'm talking about creative visualization. The power of words can help you create your destiny. There's also power in visualization – in seeing things before you accomplish them. The subconscious brain doesn't know the difference between what is real and what is vividly imagined.

Suggested actions to change your future and change your destiny.

Change your programming. That includes what we see physically and what we see in our mind's eye. Create a dream board with pictures of what you want to achieve. Your brain eventually becomes comfortable seeing these things and develops ways and means to accomplish your goals, dreams, or desires.

Visualize what you want to happen. During my morning routine, I like to meditate. While I'm meditating, I visualize. I have a story – a movie playing in my mind – with visuals and words. When you visualize, try to see and hear, even smell and feel, as if you were there. Make sure what you imagine is done with strong emotion and feeling.

So, if you want to change your future, you need to visualize. Put good things in your mind. Unfortunately, that also applies to putting negative things in your mind – if you're not edifying, uplifting, and building up, your brain will start to decay. So only put good things in it.

Visualize what you want, and you will have an incredible life!

No Traffic When You Go the Extra Mile

We all know that going the extra mile means doing more than everyone else. You're doing more than your competition, co-workers, and the people around you. You're doing more than anyone else if you're in a competitive situation, such as an athlete. You're going that extra mile.

Going the extra mile was very effective in different parts of my life. In my martial arts training, I decided early on to go all-out no matter what the others around me were doing. I chose to go that extra mile – not for the instructor, but for myself. I wasn't concerned about who was watching me – I was doing it for me. I began building my skills, training my body in the right way, and, most importantly, training my mind.

I was programming my mind to say, "You know, this guy is willing to do whatever it takes." I started to be really proud of myself – not for other people, but for me. I started internally saying, "I'm going to be really good, and I'm going to do more than anyone else." And I did! I never missed a class. I went the extra mile. Only one other person in my martial arts class surpassed me. I earned a 4th-degree black belt, and he earned a 5th-degree black belt.

I took the lesson I learned into the business world. If you can take that premise, that mindset, into your job, business, career, or whatever you're doing, you will see how you can grow and become greater than you ever expected. Your confidence in yourself will start to manifest, and you'll see tremendous success.

There is little competition when you go the extra mile and outwork everyone else. When you work harder than everyone else, you gain more self-confidence. Do it for yourself, and ultimately you will crush the competition!

The Power of Accountability and Consistency

Taking martial arts classes really helped me learn the power of accountability and consistency. Despite what others around me were doing, I went all in and didn't hold back. Whatever action was required, I did it intensely and consistently. When I wasn't feeling well, I would go to class, not intending to complete it, but would stay the whole time.

These classes were a separator for me. It wasn't about the Sensei but about having confidence in myself. I did more, was more consistent, and worked harder than anyone else. While I was accountable to someone, I was also accountable to myself.

My integrity was consistent, even when no one was watching. I watched myself and was accountable to myself and my higher power – my God. This was one of many experiences in my life that taught me that those who keep standing win.

"The Infinite Game" by Simon Sinek talks about how those who keep going will be the ones who ultimately win.

Whether you're doing sales or networking, business development, building out a company, or working a job where you want to progress within the company, be consistent—don't waiver no matter what.

If you remain, you will pass everyone over time. Go all-out! Don't "dog-it." Always do your best. Remember to be accountable to someone, but most of all, to yourself.

Find your passion and know your purpose?!

Find your passion and know your purpose?! Both the "?" and the "!" are there because it's a question *and* a statement.

I have spoken to many who believe, "If you love what you do, you'll never work a day in your life." But this is probably the biggest lie from the pit of hell. When I had my advertising company, I loved many things about it, but there were many things I really did not like about it. For example: grinding for new customers and collecting from customers who hadn't paid. Hiring was okay, but firing was not so good. So love what you do – every piece of it? On the days I wasn't loving what I was doing, I was working. So I don't believe that statement is true. You should love every piece of what you do. When I was working, I wasn't loving what I was doing.

It's important to find something you're passionate about and discover your purpose. I found "Finding Your Purpose" by Christine Whelan helpful, and it offered a lot of good information. After reading the book, I looked at my life and asked: "What is my purpose on this planet? What's going to fulfill me?"

Relying on a job, business, or career to fulfill you and your passions for 45 years is like finding a unicorn – it's impossible.

We are programmed to believe we must find this passion through our jobs. But finding your passion or purpose doesn't have to be through your work—maybe you want to do some mission work or help feed the homeless.

Here's my suggestion:

Whatever you do, use your talent and be effective at it. But use the money you're making at your job to fuel your passion instead of forcing your job to be your passion. Whatever I do, I give 120%. I am focused and driven to give my all.

I was shy, introverted, picked on, bullied, learning disabled, and dyslexic, which put me in a dark, isolated place as a young boy through my teens and into adulthood. But I've been able to break out of that shell and away from that dark place through networking, learning about self-development, and having incredible mentors. I have found my purpose, but it does not come from a job or business. So while the job can help fuel my purpose, it doesn't come from it.

My purpose: to help inspire people. I eventually want to be able to speak across the world and inspire people to help them understand that they're okay. It took me some time to accept myself, but I'm glad I did the work to become comfortable in my own skin.

That's my message to you. Find something you're passionate about and, more importantly, find your purpose.

Here's an exercise you can do (suggested by Christine in her book): create a mission statement. I created my mission statement, which helped me determine my "north star." Everything I do in my life must be pointing towards that mission statement, that purpose. I encourage you to create one and stop thinking a job is your only option. The job is important because it will enable you to earn a living and pay the bills, but ask yourself: what are you doing to make a life, and what's your purpose on this planet? Is the world going to be better because you're here?

When you go to the next phase of your life, what will others say about you at your funeral service? So definitely think about what your purpose is in life and work towards that. Be the light!

The Power of Positive Expectations

I learned many years ago from my mentors that attitude is a decision. We decide every day how we will live our lives and start our day. You can start the day with a "woe is me" mentality or an "I'm going to slay it" mentality. Or maybe it's "I'm going to go crush the day" or "punch the day in the face," or you just let the craziness of the day that is ahead overwhelm you. It really is a decision you make.

Two books on positive thinking – "The Power of Positive Thinking" by Norman Vincent Peale and "How to Stop Worrying and Start Living" by Napoleon Hill – have helped me understand and re-emphasize that power. No one wants to be around negative people. You want to be around forward-looking people with a great attitude who are jovial and happy. It's harder being with negative people.

We don't always have to be happy people. Sometimes, we share tough and challenging things, but it's how you present it – what your attitude towards it is. It really is a decision. So expect the best – whether you're going out there through networking, a business development role, or as an entrepreneur looking to grow your business or put together the right team. The Law of Attraction says that what we expect, we achieve.

In his book, "The Compound Effect," Darren Hardy describes the Law of Attraction as not being mysterious or some weird hocus-pocus type of stuff. Instead, think about it this way. You purchase a brand-new Kia and start noticing Kias everywhere – especially the model you just bought. It's because you are aware of it – you're consciously thinking about that particular car model.

So when we think about, focus on, write down, and visualize everything we want to accomplish, along with positive expectations, we start to manifest them. Our brains create grooves through the different patterns that we do and often through our actions and thoughts.

So my message is this: focus on the positive. Have positive expectations, and great things will start to come. It doesn't happen overnight. We need to regroup our thoughts through a positive expectation mindset. Following this advice can give you some incredible results.

Master of Our Fate

We are the master of our fate. A great poem by William Ernest Henley titled "Invictus" ends with: "I am the master of my fate. I am the captain of my soul."

The world we live in today has a victim-oriented, entitled mentality. But you know what? I don't believe in that. I don't buy into that at all. I believe we can create our own fate and guide our destiny, and everything we do or don't do will help us build the life we want.

I am a big believer in positive self-affirmation. I do self-talk every morning. I read. I put good things into my brain. I associate with and make sure I am around positive, forward-thinking people who are going somewhere great in life. It's important to be around spiritually-sound people, which is why I surround myself with these kinds of people.

If I'm ever the smartest guy in the room, I'm probably in the wrong room. I want to be around people who are much smarter than me because that also elevates me. So what kind of people are you associating with? What books are they reading?

What kind of self-talk are you saying to yourself? Every morning I do positive self-talk and creative visualization. I have a "movie" of what I want to accomplish that plays in my brain. Your brain is an incredible computer linked to infinite intelligence. I believe there is a spiritual force called God. When we tap into that force, great things will happen. It's also called the Law of Attraction.

When good things start happening, it's a manifestation of what's been happening over the last two to three years. It's the Law of Sowing and Reaping. What you sow, you will eventually reap. Remember, the brain is like a computer, so program only good stuff into it. The tongue is the most effective aspect of this "computer" – it's the programmer. You are programming your brain, so be strategic with your input.

It doesn't matter what was programmed earlier in your life because the great news is that you can clean out the hard drive and reprogram and repurpose your brain's computer by putting positive thoughts and words in it.

You have three really powerful sense gates — your eyes, ears, and mouth. So be deliberate about what goes out and what comes in. I am careful not to say things like (I'm uncomfortable even saying them here), "This headache is killing me." That's not a good thing to say. My mentor told me years ago, "What if everything you speak about came to fruition? Would you still say it?" So be conscious of what you think and say throughout your life.

Here's the key: you are awesome! You can be the master of your own fate. You can be the captain of your soul. It's definitely up to you! Don't put it on someone else. Take full responsibility and surround yourself with great people.

Start by answering the following questions:

- Are you a victim or a victor?
- How are you programming your brain?
- What are your daily practices?
- Who are you surrounding yourself with?
- What are you listening to?
- How are you speaking – positively or negatively, victorious or defeated?

Know this: you can do it!

It's the Little Things

It's the little things, the slightest edge, the compound effect that will create long-term success.

I believe in tracking and setting goals. I track nitty-gritty stuff now more than ever, and it's been interesting. I am finding a lot of value in it.

When you're tracking daily or regularly, it makes you accountable for yourself. Try finding someone or even a team to be accountable to. Tracking is great because it can give you these little endorphin or dopamine hits when you add your accomplishments to your tracker, and it actually makes you feel better and encourages you.

Tracking the big picture stuff, like how you did this month compared to last month, is great. While there is nothing wrong with that, I've learned that to find the ultimate goal you want to accomplish, you need to break it down month-by-month, week-by-week, day-by-day, and sometimes hour-by-hour. Break it into little tasks and little pieces, and do those little actions consistently every day because that will build and create your success.

Seeing a large obstacle blocking your dream or goal can be discouraging. But as my mentor says, "If you break it down inch by inch, everything is a cinch. But yard by yard, everything is hard."

So how do you eat an elephant? One bite at a time. You break it down into little tiny pieces. Do actions daily and regularly. Track those actions, and you will see major success over time. It's the compound effect.

For example, I lost some weight by establishing good habits and doing little things every day. Then I got off track for a while but started again with my good habits. It was three weeks of practicing these better habits before I started to see any results.

You need to have patience and give yourself grace. Eventually, if you keep the faith, you will accomplish your goal.

Don't only look at the big picture…the little things matter. Track the little things. Break down your goals into monthly, weekly, and daily actions. And keep in mind: "How do you eat an elephant – one bite at a time" and "Inch by inch, everything's a cinch, but yard by yard, it's hard."

Do You Make Resolutions, or Do You Set Goals?

Do you make resolutions, or do you set goals?

It's essential to set goals, not make resolutions. The reason: resolutions are temporary and typically only last a few weeks – if that! It's better to have a long-term vision and translate that into a long-term goal. Then, break the long-term goal down into mid-term and short-term goals with weekly and daily goals.

Your goals should be S.M.A.R.T. – Specific, Measurable, Attainable, Realistic, and Time-bound.

I don't believe in setting goals only at the end of the year. I believe in setting goals whenever you need to and breaking them down every month.

Achieving the goals you set for yourself ultimately comes down to maintaining your daily habits. "Atomic Habits" by James Clear is an excellent book about habit stacking, which is building new habits on your existing habits. Those habits will eventually create your future and destiny.

So, be sure to set goals instead of getting caught up in the hype of making resolutions.

Don't Set Resolutions, Set Goals

People often look at the new year as a time to set resolutions. Working with different mentors has taught me that resolutions are not effective. Typically, resolutions last only two weeks before a person gives up and goes back to the old patterns.

Setting manageable goals that you can keep is a better option. Setting and working toward long-term, monthly, weekly, and daily goals is the best path to success. I recommend writing down what you want to accomplish during a certain time period. One of my mentors suggests making a list of 10 things you want to accomplish. Study the list and figure out *one* thing to do. Put an action plan in place to make that goal happen. Write out what you want to accomplish in the chosen time frame. Break the plan down into daily actions, and daily habits.

The Importance of Your Appearance

In recent years, video meetings have become more common, so it's imperative that you are prepared.

Here are some subtleties to think about.

1) **Your appearance**. Consider who you are going to be speaking with, and be conscious of how you dress and how you appear to the person. (And remember to comb your hair.)

2) **Lighting**. How is your lighting? I recommend using a ring light with natural light. Make sure you are front-lit. It's crucial to have good lighting.

3) **Background**. What is your background? You don't have to use a virtual screen, but if you use a "green screen," it's more effective. Be aware of what's behind you and how your background looks.

4) **Looking at the person**. Be sure to look at the camera when you're speaking so it appears you are looking right at the other person. Otherwise, it may seem like you're not paying attention or are aloof. Also, avoid looking at your phone. If you are taking notes on your phone or on a piece of paper, let that person know so they don't think you're distracted. The key to successful video meetings is making sure the person you are speaking with feels you are engaged and interested. That's how you should make people feel because it's all about connecting. We are *not* looking to pitch – we want to *connect*. All of these suggestions make a positive difference when trying to connect with others.

The Success Journey –
Go From Grit to Grind to Glory

What does the journey to success look like for you?

To achieve success, you must go from grit to grind before you get to glory.

I surround myself with people who are successful or are on the success journey, trying to achieve it.

People make too many excuses about what's happening to them that is preventing "success." I'm not being insensitive, and I challenge you to have grit!

You must be able to go through the crap. You need to have grit! Whatever you say you're going to do, you need to do it and stick with it – no excuses!

In the martial arts, I received numerous injuries that required stitches all over my face, including a really bad broken nose, but I never missed a class. I made it and went on to get two black belts.

I never quit! I didn't "take a break." You have to be gritty!

I love the following explanation of "grit."

You need to have "inte-GRITty ("integrity")! You have to be gritty, but the grit is actually doing what you say you're going to do! Follow through, and have the integrity to do it!

After you get through the grit, stay in the grind. Embrace the grind – keep going!

I've learned that you've got to love the grind. Embrace the process. Embrace the suck, and eventually, the glory – whatever you're striving for – will come!

For me, success is a journey, not a destination. It's not something you're eventually going to hit, and that's the end of it. There's always something else to strive for.

But you'll only get the recognition, the glory, whatever that glory is, if you go through the grit and the grind. Eventually, if you do these things, the glory will come…whatever glory looks like to you.

So what does glory mean to you?

The Secret of the Corn

Have you heard the "secret of the corn?"

No, it's not a horror flick. It's the universal idea that relates to seed time, progression time, and harvest time.

We want success to happen now! But – what are your answers to these questions?

- Are you planting seeds consistently?

- Are you putting in the work?

- Are you doing the work needed to create positive results?

Imagine if you were at a large area of land in the Midwest and said, "Okay, land – give me crops, give me corn." Ah, no – there are steps you need to take before you can harvest a crop. Prepare the soil. Plant the seeds. And not just one seed, but lots of them.

The same applies to contacting potential customers – you can't talk to that person once and expect immediate results. You need to plant a lot of seeds, fertilize them, and nurture them along the way.

If you plant the seeds in the spring, you won't see stalks coming up until fall. How many kernels are on each ear of corn? How many ears of corn are on each stalk? Think about how much corn one little seed creates.

But to see ears of corn, it takes time and work. Your business requires that you are willing to put in the work consistently.

So let's talk about consistency. It takes about six months for the corn to grow from start to finish – seed to progression to harvest. So when looking at what you're doing today, think about what you did six months ago. Did you plant seeds then that are ready to be harvested today? If you don't have success right now, ask yourself, what were you doing six months ago?

I choose to plant seeds every single day because I want every single day to have a harvest!

So be consistent, pay attention to the "secret of the corn," and you can have success too!

Are You Emptying Your Cup?

When starting a new venture, entrepreneurs will often meet with a coach and come to the table with a lot of knowledge and preconceived ideas.

Todd Stottlemyre, in his book, "Relentless Success," tells a story about a young man who had trained in the martial arts for many years. He heard about this great master, so he traveled all the way through China barefoot, worked for weeks, and finally made it to the master's home. He knocked on the door and introduced himself as the master opened the door.

He said, "Master, I'd love to be able to talk to you. Maybe you'd consider training me?" The master cordially invited him inside the home, and they sat down for tea. As he was preparing the tea, the young man kept reciting his theories on the martial arts, his experiences, his perspective, his philosophy, and the things he's done.

The old master was humble and friendly. He kept smiling and nodding his head. Then the master asked the young man if he'd like some tea. The young man nodded and continued speaking. As the master poured the tea, it started to overflow the cup. The young man became distracted and blurted out, "Master! The cup is full!" And the master answered, 'Yes, my son. The cup is full. Just like the cup, if your mind is full, you cannot receive any more."

The metaphor is that you have a lot of information in your head. When you go to a mentor or coach, you need to go with an "empty cup" rather than lots of ideas and information. We live in an information age with access to all kinds of data that can give the illusion that we have all the information needed.

If you plan to learn from someone who's been there and done that, who has experience, it is essential to go with an empty cup. Try to rid yourself of all of the noise and any preconceived notions before coming to the table.

You may be surprised at how much you will grow personally and professionally when you do. Be in the moment – empty your cup.

Life and Death Exist in the Tongue

The tongue is very powerful – life and death can be in the tongue.

Recently, I was listening to a voicemail where the caller made a comment that it didn't sound like his voice.

We hear our voices through our inner ears. We don't hear it on the outside like we hear other people's voices. The inner ear is linked to our subconscious and our intelligence – our superior or infinite intelligence whom some people call God or a higher power.

The tongue is very powerful. It programs you and others around you. It's like a ship's rudder; it is small but provides direction. The tongue acts like the keyboard to the most powerful computer in the world – your brain!

Try this: speak on and think about something completely different than what you are currently focused on. You can't do it. It's impossible! What we are speaking about is what we're focused on, what we're thinking about. If you want to be positive, move forward, and have great things happen in your life, you have to speak it. Continually doing that will help reprogram our minds and help to dilute some of the negative things that happen in our lives.

We also know that words can affect other people and relationships. Once you say something aloud to another person, there's no way to take it back. The analogy given was if you were in a car driving and you throw one thousand $1 bills out the window of a moving car, the wind would take them in different directions, making it impossible to pick them all up. Once the words leave your mouth, you can't take them back. You can try to make amends, but the words can't be recalled, so be very conscious of what you say.

My mentor says to me, "Let me ask you a question: if everything you say came to pass, would you watch what you say more closely?" It's an interesting idea to think about. So many times, we say things to ourselves like, "Oh man, I am really bad at spelling!" You don't want to program yourself that way.

I have a friend who is raising his daughter. She is a little reserved, and when people call her shy, he says, "No, please don't program me or my daughter with that language." Maybe she is cautious, which doesn't make her shy. I think I was shy and introverted because I was programmed to believe I was.

So, be very conscious of what you think and say. It will program you and others.

Without a Vision, People Perish

What's your vision? What's your "why"? What motivates you?

You need to have a vision. King Solomon said, "Where there is no vision, the people perish." (Proverbs 29:18)

You need to know what you want. You need to know what your "why" is and what your long-term vision is.

There's so much talk today about the "what." What am I going to do? What kind of job or business? Don't focus on that. I've learned through incredible mentors in my life to know your "why" first.

The "who" is finding the people in your life who can help you with your "why." Maybe it's a team or a mentor or a coach.

Don't focus on the "what" because when the "why" is clear, the "who" will show up, and the "what" and the "how" will magically appear.

Go all-in with your "why" and your vision! When you actively follow your vision and your purpose, the universe will cooperate.

Persistence is Stubbornness with a Purpose

What is your superpower? Mine is persistence. I don't have a "quit" bone in my body, and I don't know how to stop. You may have heard you need a high IQ (intelligence quotient) to succeed. Well, I'm here to dispel that theory.

I have a low IQ ("I Quit") because I don't know how to quit. My persistence and never-quit attitude is the reason I got two martial arts black belts and passed all but one student in my dojo (martial arts studio). I can tell you numerous stories, both personally and throughout history about people who didn't give up.

Look at Thomas Edison... it took him 10,000 attempts before he perfected the light bulb. Rather than accepting failure 9,999 times, he is quoted as saying this regarding his failures: "I have not failed. I have just found 9,999 ways that do not work." That man had a purpose and persisted until he succeeded!

Persistence is great because if you don't quit, you win! But you must have a purpose, a mission, and know what your real reason is.

I've heard this said, and it really resonated with me: "In the absence of purpose, people pleasure seek." We've seen a lot of that in the last few months. Having a purpose, being stubbornly persistent, and persevering will allow you to achieve the success you're looking for.

Make What Brings You Life a Priority

Someone once said to me, "What brings you life? Make it a priority in your life." I had to share it because it's awesome!

What fires you up?
What brings you life?
What motivates you?

Once you find it, make it a priority! It may be your business, a job, or a career. It may not be. I put together a life mission statement that really moves me; it drives and motivates me. Whatever I am doing must align with my life mission statement. Any money I earn will support that mission statement because it brings my life joy.

Younger folks are scattered and don't know how to prioritize. It's challenging for them, but it must be done. We all can do multiple things in our life; we just need to do them one at a time. Avoid doing three things simultaneously, but you can do three things in one day. Consider spending three hours focused on one thing, the next three hours focused on another thing, and another three hours on something else.

Without prioritizing, nothing will get done. It's not going to happen, so I strongly recommend prioritizing what brings your life. You have to first know what that is to make it a priority.

To prioritize, utilize one of the best tools you have: the calendar on your phone. It's simple to use and can alert you when you have a task to complete. For me, if it's not on my calendar, it's not getting done. I live and die by my calendar.

So, whatever is important to you in life, make it a priority! Find your passion, focus, and prioritize to get there.

Is Success *Hard* or Is It *Heart?*

Success is heart – not hard, but heart. It's not about how hard you work. It's about doing it with all your heart – with the right heart!

Is your heart in the right place? Is it in a place where you want to help others and make a difference, make an impact? If you're self-focused, success is hard because people don't want to get behind you when they think it's about you. But when it's about others, people are more willing to join your team. They want to join the party; they become supporters.

It's about the heart you put into it. It's easy to just go through the motions, but it's another thing to give it all you've got. I heard a story about an athlete who broke the record for the high jump. The bar was much higher than anyone had jumped over before. When asked how he did it, he answered, "Well, I threw my heart over the bar, and the rest of my body followed."

Give it all you got – it takes heart to succeed. So give your heart to whatever you're doing. Be a go-giver. Don't make it about you – be others-focused. This shift in mindset has changed my life. Make it about loving what you're doing because you are making an impact on this world.

Success is Not Always About Addition. Sometimes It's About Subtraction

What are you willing to give up to achieve success?

Success is not always about adding more and more stuff; sometimes, it's about taking away. What can you subtract from your life?

The many distractions in our lives and our various activities often slow us down. It could be over the top in social media activity or watching too much Netflix. Maybe it's too many personal or family commitments. I'm all about family, but maybe there's too much happening.

Look at what is most important to you, determine what you need to achieve to succeed, and make it your priority. A mentor of mine told me, "If what you're doing is not taking you straight to your goal, then it's going to take you off course."

We have two assets: our time and money. How are you spending or investing your time? How are you spending or investing your money? Are your spending and investing getting you closer to your goals? If not, then stop. If you do this, success will happen. It's there for you!

There's No Elevator to Success.
Take the Stairs

There's no elevator to success. You will need to take the stairs.

Success is a journey. It won't happen by signing up for something, like joining the gym, and then boom - you're successful, or in this case, you're in shape! You will encounter obstacles and experience challenges. You will have struggles that you will have to overcome, and it's okay!

Success doesn't happen by proxy. Being around successful people won't make you successful. You have to do the work and grind it out. Make sure you're doing whatever you need to do to succeed. I want to tell you straight up – you can do it!

Having the right resources is essential. Consider finding someone who can mentor you, someone who's been there, done that. Someone who has taken the road less traveled. If you're going to walk through a minefield, do you want to be last or first? You want to be last! You want to walk in a leader's exact footprints. In fact, you may even want to figure out the exact same style and size of shoes to squeeze into so you don't get blown up!

My advice: have someone in your life as a mentor. Do the work. Grind it out every day. Surround yourself with a positive network of people who will support and encourage you. Always put the good stuff in you to strengthen your resolve. Challenges and struggles will try to throw you off, but if you're always putting in the right stuff, that will help put you in a good frame of mind.

In the movie, "Finding Nemo," Dory says, "Just keep swimming!" So keep going, keep swimming, because success is imminent!

Do You Want Success?
You've Got to Get Gritty!

Do you want to be successful? Do you want success? You've got to be gritty! You've got to have grit! You are bred to be a champion! You need to believe that!

I heard a story (but I'm not sure who the author is) about a young man who went to a guru and said, "I really want to know the secret to success." The guru asked, "You really want to know?" He replied, "Yeah, I really want to know." So the guru said, "Let's take a walk." So they walked to the beach. While chatting, they started walking into the water until it became chin deep. Then the guru said, "You really want to know the secret of success?" He said, "Yes, I do really want to know." "You're sure? You trust me?" "Yes!" The guru pushed the young man's head under the water. The young man starts flailing his arms, and finally, the guru lets him up. Sputtering, the young man asks, "Are you crazy? What did you do that for?" His answer: "Listen, the minute you want to succeed as much as you want oxygen, you'll succeed."

So, you need to have grit to deal with whatever comes up in your life. One of the reasons why I'm so blessed is that I have a mentor in my life who has helped me with both business and personal issues. The biggest thing that prevents us from succeeding is life stuff that holds us down – like family challenges. We want to succeed so that we can help our families. When challenges come, make them the reason, not the excuse!

Having grit helps you get through challenges so you will succeed. Don't be wishy-washy. Don't be that fish that is floating in the water. A dead fish floats with the current, but live fish swim against it! We want to be going against or with the tide, whatever is needed, to succeed. We need to be gritty!

Your Self-Worth Will Equal Your Net Worth

Do you ever wonder why you don't have the net worth you want? Well, it's simple... your self-worth is directly proportional to your net worth. How you feel about yourself eventually will manifest in what you will be worth. So make sure you're constantly growing yourself.

I have a crazy background with very low self-esteem for many years (picked on, bullied, learning disabled, dyslexic), but through a lot of personal growth, reading books, surrounding myself with the right kinds of people, having a mentor in my life, continually putting good things in my brain, and honestly by out-working everyone, I have been able to grow my self-worth.

Grow you, and you will grow your income and, ultimately, your net worth. Make sure to always work on these three things:

1. Grow yourself through self-development. Read positive mental attitude (PMA) books, listen to success-oriented audios, be around successful, success-minded people, and have a mentor in your life.

2. Out-work the competition and maintain a strong, consistent work ethic.

3. Continuously serve others. By helping people, you make a difference in their lives. They will tell you how much you impact them, which will grow your self-image.

Continually look to grow your self-worth, and you'll see your net worth grow.

Success is a Very Poor Teacher

Success is a very poor teacher. That sounds strange, but it's true! We think that success will breed success, and to a degree, it does. However, the stumbling blocks, the failures that happen in our life that we learn from, make us better.

I read "The Cashflow Quadrant" by Robert Kiyosaki, which contains many great nuggets. He tells the story of how he acquired a real estate deal and brought it to his dad, who basically tore it apart. But through his mistakes in that initial transaction, he learned a lot. He restructured the deal correctly, and it ended up good for him.

For me, I got my nose busted big time in martial arts. My Sensei was coming at me with a flurry of kicks, and his knee came right into my nose and destroyed it! I learned what to do when that happened again. I've had a lot of stitches on my eyebrows, under my eyes, my lip – all this crazy stuff from martial arts. But through those experiences, I kept going and learned what not to do and what to do better.

Don't be afraid to fail. Many of my life and business lessons have enhanced my success through some failures. One of my mentors, who is uber-successful, said this to me: "When you fail as much as I have, you will have the kind of success and lifestyle that I have."

Don't shy away from failure. Fail forward and get up. Learn from it and keep going.

Harvest Time is Coming Soon

Karma. Good energy. I don't know what your beliefs are. I believe in God as my Higher Power. I believe that when you give good, you get good; when you speak good words, good words come back to you.

What is harvest time? You sow, as in planting, till the soil, look after it, and eventually, you reap. There's planting, seed time, progression time, and harvest time. For me, right now, it's harvest time. Sometimes you are planting and tending to the grunt work and may not feel good about doing those tasks, but it does come.

You may already know my story – a shy, introverted kid from the Bronx who comes from humble beginnings, divorced parents, living hand-to-mouth, and not the best environment for success. But it changed when I put myself around good people, spoke good words, and continued to work toward doing the right thing. Now things are starting to happen. Harvest time is here, and it's really neat to see.

I'm saying all this so you understand that your time is coming. I want you to understand and believe that. If it doesn't happen right away, don't get frustrated. Galatians 6:9 says, "Don't get weary in well-doing, but in due season you will reap." Be faithful. Do the work. Your time is coming.

Plan for a six-month window between when you put the seed in the ground and when the harvest happens, and ensure you're faithful in those six months. Plant good seeds during that time to get a good harvest. That's why I've always tried – not perfect at it, but I try – to plant good seeds. Sow good consistently so you can reap good.

Stay steady. Stay faithful. Trust the process, and good things will come for you.

Crazy...or Destined for Greatness?

Are you crazy, or are you destined for greatness? When you are looking to succeed at a high level, you will get tomatoes thrown at you, and people will think you're crazy or fanatical. Consider that "fan" is a derivative of "fanatical." When you're trying to do something extraordinary in your life, it's a little crazy. But if you stick with it and don't allow yourself to quit, you will succeed.

However, you must have a purpose for trying to do something great. You need an overarching, big reason or goal for doing it. If it's just something different or unique, that won't be enough to drive you—have a purpose!

I wrote a life mission statement that I abide by and live by. I've heard this quote: "In the absence of a purpose, people pleasure seek." And I've been there; I'm just as guilty as anyone. We want to pleasure seek. We want to do the things that make us feel good, but it's only temporary, not what success is.

Success is grinding it out. The first three letters of success are s-u-c (suck). You've got to go through the "suck" to get to success. I always say this: "You don't quit; you win. You don't quit; you succeed." Another good quote I've heard is, "Age wrinkles the body, but quitting wrinkles the soul." Put that in your heart and soul and think about it.

Here's another one: "Success doesn't have sympathy for the validity of your circumstances." We tend to allow ourselves to make excuses, like: "I'm too busy" or "I'm shy and introverted." Don't let yourself off the hook. You can do it! You can do anything you put your mind to by getting fanatical, and you've got to get a little crazy.

Do the things that others aren't willing to do. I saw a video where Kobe Bryant talked about getting up 3-4 hours earlier than the top-level players in the NBA. He knew that over time, he would separate himself big time. And he certainly did. So get a little crazy. Don't worry about what others think. Don't worry about everyone else. You do what you know is right.

Make sure you have a purpose and know where you're going. Make sure there's a big reason why you're doing it. Doing something because it's cool or different will not be enough to sustain you.

You will succeed; you are destined for greatness! See you at the top!

The Story of the Chinese Bamboo Tree

I want to tell you the story of the Chinese bamboo tree…

Many people, including me, start to lose a little faith. You think, "I've been doing this work, and I'm not where I want to be." You feel like you've been grinding it out and just working, working, working… but it's not happening yet. Think about people like Steve Jobs, Warren Buffet, or Elon Musk. Their "overnight success" took 20 years of grinding.

Success takes time, and you must build a foundation for that success. Some of us, me for sure, need to grow from within. I needed a lot of internal growth to be a better version of who I was. My lack of people skills was a challenge—I didn't have any. I was shy, introverted, and bullied. I added martial arts later in life. Back then, I'd prefer to "hit" you than talk to you or relate to you or be friends with you. I didn't participate in team sports growing up; I did individual sports, like karate, tennis, and chess.

Fundamentally, I didn't know how to work with others. I had confidence issues and would look at others and think they were much better than me. I was critical of myself and lacked confidence. Whatever the challenge is, however, I've learned that we need to start from within. I am a huge proponent of self-development and mentorship because things help you grow and become the best version you can be. People lose sight of success, thinking it's about learning business tactics and techniques. Those things contribute to success, but we must first grow and develop ourselves.

I'm mentioning all of this because it relates to the story of the Chinese bamboo tree. Here's how it works: You plant the bamboo seed. You water and fertilize the soil. You tend to it. You make sure it's doing okay. You do that for a year, and nothing happens. You tend to it for another year, and again nothing happens. In year three, you do the work – nothing.

Year four – nothing. You start questioning if anything is going to happen. The start of the fifth year – nothing. Then around the ninth week of year five, it shoots up 90 feet!

So the obvious question is: Did it grow 90 feet in just those nine weeks? The answer is no. It was growing all along, and it was creating the root system to be able to sustain something that shoots up 90 feet. Think about it – if it shoots up 90 feet with no stability, it will fall over quickly or be unable to withstand the wind when it blows. So it had to create that kind of root system, a strong foundation.

The Chinese bamboo tree concept can apply to us in life and success. The point is: don't lose faith. Don't look at what's on the outside. Understand that there is growth happening within you. This is to inspire you and be the light that says you can do it! You just need to remain steady and faithful while working on yourself.

I've heard this said: "Don't confuse the complexity of growing you with the simplicity of growing your business or becoming successful." You need to do several things, however, to make that happen. You shouldn't do what I've seen others do: "When I get it all right, then I'll start." No, that's like saying to a fireplace, "You give me the heat, then I'll give you the wood." Or saying, "I need to clean myself before showering." Or "I need to get in shape before I start karate." Start karate; then you'll get in shape.

The growth happens when you're doing. Growing you is super important! Don't neglect it. You can do it! But you have to do the work and be consistent. Grow you, and you will be successful. Remember, you must build the foundation before sustainable success can happen. It may take five, ten, or twenty years, but people will still claim you were an overnight success. You, however, will know the truth... you are that Chinese bamboo tree.

Farmers Don't Cram Their Crops

Farmers don't cram when it comes to their crops. What am I talking about? You've heard the term you must sow before you reap. We often have the perspective and mentality that we can do something last minute or quickly and expect immediate results.

Think about it. Farmers are sowing at the end of August, hoping that there will be a crop by the end of September–October. They're planting it months before, doing the prep work in early spring. Then seed time, progression time, and harvest time.

Many people want success in their business quickly. They want it now, but it doesn't happen that way. You must put in the work. You can't do something for a short time and expect results; that's not how success works.

Stay steady. I've heard: "The sign of maturity doesn't come with age; it comes from taking responsibility." You must take responsibility in advance. Be diligent and ensure you're sowing the seed consistently—not sporadically. Let's say there's a six-month period for the sowing and reaping process. So you sow, and six months later, you reap. But what about in-between? You want to sow consistently so that you can reap consistently.

Do the work. Sow, but don't expect it to happen right away. Be patient. Over time the results will come. If you stay steady and don't quit, you will succeed. I'm telling you that you can do it!

Get Your BSA Degree…Believe, Speak, Act

Get your BSA degree! It's not about getting a college degree. BSA stands for believe, speak, and act. It's about getting the biggest and best room – the room for self-improvement.

Believe

What do you believe? How are you using your belief? Faith is the substance of things hoped for and the evidence of things not seen. You've got to believe. Know in your heart of hearts, deep in your soul! As I've often said, "If you don't quit, you win." Just know you're going to win. Believe it! You are designed for greatness. God doesn't make junk. I believe He created us and engineered us for greatness.

Speak

Speak victory! Speak what you want, not what you don't want. "I'm going to win this. I'm going to succeed. I'm going to get that job or promotion." Just keep repeating it. Speak it with belief.

Act

You can speak and believe all you want, but nothing will happen if you don't act. If you don't move, nothing happens. Faith without works is dead. God doesn't steer parked cars. You've got to take action. Farmers don't miraculously think a crop will grow without acting on it.

BSA

Believe in your heart and soul and every fiber of your being. Speak what you want and speak it consistently. Then take action regularly. Do these things, and over time, you will see successful results.

How Much Discipline is Required to Succeed?

Is a lot of discipline required to succeed? No. And here's what I mean. I read an incredible book, "The One Thing" by Gary Keller and Jay Papasan. One great takeaway from the book is that not a lot of sustained discipline is required to succeed.

You need a lot of discipline for a short period to develop a habit. As noted by the authors, the number of days to create a habit is 66 days, not 21 or 30 days, as others suggest. You need enough discipline to grind it out so that the habit is formed.

Success is inevitable if you figure out that one thing you need to do to succeed and create that habit.

Do You Have Great Expectations?

Do you have great expectations? I'm not talking about the book by Charles Dickens; I'm talking about how you want to have great expectations regarding success. Do you have a positive expectancy for success? You want to expect the best things.

I heard a story about an experiment where rats were separated into two groups. One group was told their set of rats was incredible and gave them a task. The other group was told that their rats were just average. The results: the rats in the "extra special" group well exceeded the performance of the "normal" rats.

A similar study was done with students. Teachers were told that a specific group of students were geniuses and very bright, and those students performed well above the average GPA.

So what's the point? The point is expectation. You always want to think and expect the best. If you're looking for that new promotion, expect it. Yes, you have to do the work but expect the best results. Expect great things, and great things will happen. That's the power of having "great expectations," Anyone can succeed if they set their minds to it.

Chasing Your Dreams

Are you chasing your dreams, or is a nightmare chasing you?

What is your why?

What keeps the fuel in your tank?

What makes you get out of bed in the morning with excitement?

What gives you a pep in your step?

If you haven't read it (lately), I recommend the book, "Start with Why" by Simon Sinek.

Have you crystallized your why?

Do you speak it daily?

Do you have pictures up?

Do you visualize it daily?

Do you have daily goals set to achieve your dream?

Crazy People Talk to Themselves...
Do They Really?

What do you say when you talk to yourself? What's your self-talk or the soundtracks playing inside of your head?

We all have an internal dialogue inside our heads. You can't get rid of them, but you can replace them. You can program yourself for failure or success!

Some of the dialogue that I heard in my head was, "You're too small," "You're not that smart," and "What makes you think you can do that?" "What makes you so special?"

But I overrode those dialogues with positive affirmations like: "I am a champion," "I am a winner," and "I can do all things through Him who strengthens me."

Can you relate?

We all have scripts and thoughts going on in our brains. We need to control those thoughts, and the only way to do that is by programming ourselves. Come up with positive scripts. I recommend reading "Soundtracks" by Jon Acuff and "What to Say When You Talk to Yourself" by Shad Helmstetter on how to do that. They are tremendous and will help you!

Four Pillars

Pillar #1 – Overcoming Obstacles

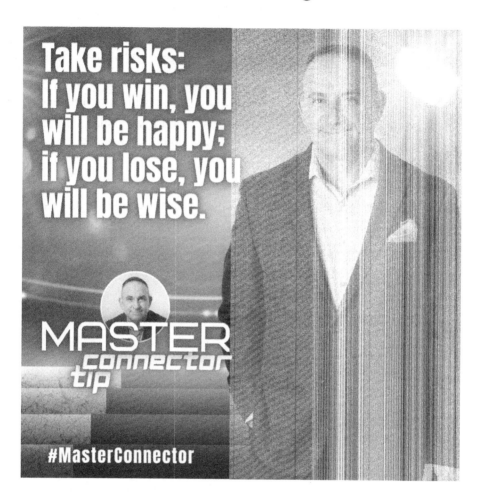

Take risks:
If you win, you
will be happy;
if you lose, you
will be wise.

MASTER
connector
tip

#MasterConnector

Introduction by Scott Ferguson

Grit is a monotonous activity essential to success in all pillars of your life, whether it be work, money, living environment, personal growth, health, recreation, community, family, or God. Each pillar will show its gnarly teeth at some point in your life. In my good friend and colleague Steve Spiro's book, *The Tao of the Master Connector*, he lays out step-by-step actions to take to Level UP your life in each area.

Like myself, Steve has studied the martial arts, and you must utilize Grit daily to make improvements. I've been taught that "inch by inch, it's a cinch; by the yard, it's hard." Steve breaks down how to rid yourself of the baggage and find the light to lighten the load that may be holding you back. Steve is also of the understanding that you either win or learn. Setbacks will happen, and there are lessons in each and every one of them.

I feel grateful Steve wrote this book as I respect him immensely, and I picked up so many Knowledge Nuggets to add to my persistence and Grit protocol.

Thank you, Steve!

Scott Ferguson

Introduction by Ramon Ray

Challenges and difficulties are an absolutely expected part of life, which we simply can't avoid. In fact, we should embrace it.

In *The Tao of a Master Connector*, Steve shares the importance of focusing on what you HAVE and not on what you don't have. When you're faced with a challenge, inventory your assets.

Consider what you have right. Focus on what you have, build upon these things, and use them to overcome the challenge.

Other principles Steve touches on are "faith" and "fear." Faith is the blind ambition that children have, making them feel they can do anything. Sometimes not knowing that you're "supposed to fail" helps you succeed.

When I launched my first big event series in 2006, I had never done something that big—an event with hundreds of people and national, household-name sponsors. Faith and belief helped me overcome my fear. I didn't have someone to tell me I couldn't do it. I had the BELIEF that I could, and I went on to successfully produce the event many years after and before successfully selling it.

So, FAITH in yourself and belief in YOU is essential!

Ramon Ray

Pillar #1 Introduction –
Having the Grit to Overcome Obstacles

I want to speak about having the grit to overcome obstacles and challenges because we all have many challenges in our life. Some of the lessons I've learned are shared in the stories and parables in this section.

If you stick to something and don't quit, you will win. In some of these stories, the message is that you can succeed, and everything will be okay because you have what it takes.

Through my martial arts experience, I learned I could pass everyone in my class because I had the grit to overcome obstacles. Despite breaking my nose, requiring stitches on my face several times, and broken bones, I hung in there and stuck with it!

The secret to success is having the grit to overcome obstacles and challenges; hopefully, the stories in this section will bless you!

Start with What You've Got Right Now!

One lesson I've learned from incredible people in my life is to do it now! Don't wait! In fact, when I was doing a lot more driving, I posted a note that said, "Do it now!" on my steering wheel.

My mentor tells me, "Entrepreneurs act. They don't overthink or over-evaluate." I read "The Magic of Thinking Big" by David J. Schwartz, which talks about some success diseases like detail-I and procrastination. We tend to sit and wait because we want all the details and information before we think we can move. But honestly, it doesn't work like that.

If you are married, did you have all the details of what your spouse would be like before you were married? Probably not. There were many things you had to address along the way. Or what about picking your college? There was a lot you didn't know, but you went anyway.

People often get stuck. I know – I've been there! We tend to want to overanalyze. So, my message is simple and short: You are good where you are. You don't need to have all the information. You don't need to be perfect. I tried to be this perfect person for many years, but we will never be perfect. We must be the best version of ourselves, which will happen along the journey.

Great people have taught me, "The learning is in the doing." You get good by doing, and you learn while doing. You try, fail, adjust, try, fail, adjust. Eventually, success will happen. Sometimes it may not be exactly as you thought it would be, and you have to start and see what happens. Don't overthink! Don't make it complicated. You are good right now!

If you're considering doing more on social media, just start. Do something! Doing something is better than nothing. The "Great One,"

Wayne Gretzky, said, "I missed 100% of the shots I did not take." So, take a shot and don't worry about it. If you do, you have a 50/50 chance of succeeding. If you don't, you have a 100% chance of failing! Throw caution to the wind, and you'll find that action cures fears. If you're afraid, have anxiety, or trepidation, the best thing to do is to take action. That's how I started doing my *Fired Up Friday* series videos on LinkedIn and have encouraged many others to create videos.

Successful entrepreneurs act. They live by the mindset of "ready, fire, aim." If you're looking to do more about connecting with people or attending more traditional networking events – try it! Make that call – do it! Take action – you'll do great!

Time Management or Event Management?

My mentor taught me that we never manage time; it just ticks away for 24 hours each day. No matter what we do, we can't make it 26 hours. We only have 24 hours per day, seven days per week. We can, however, manage the events or schedules in our lives, which is why it's so important to block out time.

Consider this analogy about a professor who taught his students a lesson to make his point. The students in his class complained that they didn't have enough time to study or finish their homework. So, one day, he brought a large glass beaker and a large bowl of rocks to class. He put the rocks in the beaker and asked the class, "Is the beaker full?" Everyone said, "Yes." He then added some smaller pebbles, which fit in between the crevices of the larger rocks. And again, he asked if it was full, and many students said it was. Then he poured gravel into the beaker and asked the question again. Then he added some sand. He asked if the beaker was full, and everyone said yes. Finally, he grabbed a pitcher of water and poured it in. Then he said, "Now the beaker is officially full."

Many people don't take control of their schedule. They first let the sand, gravel, and pebbles in, so fitting the larger rocks in is impossible.

I was taught that the larger rocks are the essential things in our lives – what we're trying to accomplish. I've also heard it noted as future-based events – something that will move your life forward. It could be relational or spiritual, and it could be work, job, or business-related. It is important to make time for the important things first.

I have a policy in my family and my life: I live and die by my calendar. If it's not on my calendar, I don't do it. I create calendar events for everything I need to do. For example, I was working on losing weight but hadn't gotten out to do cardio. My sister, who's my coach, asked me if it was on my calendar. I hadn't been putting it on my calendar, so it wasn't happening. If it's on my calendar, it's getting done.

One thing that I've found very effective is sending out calendar invites. I send out a calendar invite if I need to schedule with somebody, and I will put it on my calendar even if it's a 10-minute phone call. Hopefully, you're also doing that because it's a very effective tool. I set most of my appointments for 30 minutes using a calendar app called "Calendly." I have specific settings within that app that make sense and are helpful to me.

Some good tools are available to help you manage the events in your life, and I recommend using them to help you move your life forward.

Feeding Two Monsters – Fear or Faith

Consider these two monsters: fear and faith.

You feed one or the other, depending on your thoughts and actions.

Are you thinking and focusing on fear? Are you focusing on what may or may not happen?

Or are you putting your focus on faith and belief? Are you focusing on knowing and expecting positive results?

In. this context, we're not talking about religious faith but about expectations. Often, we say, "I'll believe it when I see it." But that's not true faith.

Faith is seeing something in your mind's eye before it happens or believing something positive will happen. It is the substance of things not seen but the hope of things still to come. You have to believe! I've learned that whatever you're feeding will get the most attention.

Let me share a Native American story about two wolves – a black wolf and a white wolf.

The black wolf represents dark forces, while the white wolf represents light. The wolves start fighting. Which one will win? The answer: the one that is being fed. Not the hungry one – not the one who hasn't been fed for a while, making it starving and desperate. But the one who has been fed because it is strong and able to overcome the other.

That's why it's important to feed faith. It will make you stronger and empower you. If you feed fear, that will only increase fear in your world.

So, feed faith, not fear.

Losses or Lessons...Winning or Learning...

Are you ever afraid to make a mistake?

Do you feel like if you fail, you'll never succeed?

I read a really good book called "Mindset, The New Psychology of Success" by Carol S. Dweck, Ph.D., which I highly recommend. It talks about having a fixed mindset vs. a growth mindset. I had a fixed mindset, and sometimes I feared making mistakes, saying the wrong thing, or failing.

Success is failure turned inside out.

You must fail in order to succeed—the way not to succeed is by quitting.

So, make sure you're turning losses into lessons. If you lose, figure out what you learned from it. What can you pick up from those losses?

Most people think you're either winning or losing. No, you're either winning or learning.

Choose a different perspective. Don't be afraid to make mistakes or not always win. Learn from these experiences. Take what you can, evaluate it, and determine what you can do better next time.

That's what champions do. They get over stuff, learn from it, and continue to grow and refine.

Use each failure as an opportunity to get better.

If you embrace what I'm saying, you will have long-term success.

It's Time to Get Light and Lose the Baggage

Do you ever feel bogged down?

Do you feel like there's a lot of weight on your shoulders? Guilt or shame or self-judgment?

It's time to get light and lose the baggage!

Trust me; I've been there! There was a time in my life when I was in a very dark place.

I was carrying around shame from being bullied, guilt from things I had done, and guilt about what I hadn't accomplished. The voices in my head told me, "You're a loser; you can't do this, you can't do that."

I played the judgment game by looking at other people and thinking they were more successful, better-looking, or funnier than me.

I'm here to tell you that you need to lose all of that!

Usually, you don't want your baggage lost when traveling, but in this case, it's a good thing to lose the baggage – lose all that negative stuff and get light!

Forgive yourself and forgive others.

Get the help you need, whether it's spiritual or psychological.

Let's be the type of people who serve others. It's hard to be a blessing to others when you're bogged down with negative thinking. It's time to move on!

Now is the time to get reignited. Believe you are amazing because you are!

Get light so you can be a light to others.

It's Hard to Hit a Target If You Keep Moving It

It's tough to hit a target if you keep moving it!

What do I mean? Many times, people are looking for the "next new thing," or the "next big thing," or the "newest technique." Or this business or this job or this promotion. We tend to think the grass is greener on the other side.

If you're doing that, constantly moving the target, it will be really hard to hit the bullseye.

My wife and I tried ax throwing—it was a blast! But if that target had been moving, it would have been difficult for me to hone in on hitting the bullseye.

Staying focused and steady with what you have in place is important. Then you can start to refine and eventually hit that target.

Instead of looking at other things, extensions, or outside influences, ensure you're being intentionally focused. If you do that, you will be successful over time. It's not an overnight thing or a get-rich-quick scheme.

Success will not happen overnight – it takes time and work. It will require refining, being better, always growing, and being the best version of yourself. But you can't do that if you keep moving around.

Work with your coach (hopefully, you have one) and dial in on what it will take to succeed. Remember, every time you change, you start from scratch again.

Consider this analogy: metaphorically, you're on a train, and success is the journey. Often, we become impatient, thinking that success should be at the next stop, and if it isn't, we get off the train at the stop called frustration. But what if success was only three stops away?

Stay steady! Success is coming if you stay on the right train!

It's Only Impossible Until Someone Actually Does It

Have you ever said, "I can't do it!"

Have you ever said, "I need to see it to believe it?"

Well, sometimes it's only impossible until "someone" does it…

Why can't you be that "someone"?

We're often so bogged down by our self-conceptions, limitations, and things we think we can or can't do. Isn't it interesting that when suddenly "someone" does it, we feel like maybe we can do it too?

Consider the story of Roger Bannister. For years, many people, including medical doctors, said that it was impossible to run a 4-minute mile. They cited many reasons and stated that it could not be done. But Roger Bannister, who happened to be a doctor, did it! Soon after, many people also broke the 4-minute mile barrier. It's normal now for those who want to do it.

There are so many other areas in life, business, and success where people have proven the "impossible" can be accomplished. The key: don't limit yourself! Most of the time, it comes down to what we think and how we program our brains.

I heard a quote recently that really blew my mind. It's simple: "The only enemy is the inner me."

Often, we are our own worst enemies. We need to focus on being alive and believing in ourselves that anything is possible. It's scriptural. It's a success principle.

Now, I'm not talking about being unrealistic. For example, if I say I'm going to become an oak tree, that's obviously not going to happen.

But in terms of success or accomplishments, anything is possible. You must believe that you can do it. It starts with your mind convincing your body, then your body starts moving in the right direction, and eventually, it happens.

Here's your challenge: Believe in yourself to be the first record or barrier-breaker. Don't wait for someone else to do it – you do it first!

Know that you can do it!

Go Through the "Suck" to Get to Success

How do you go through the suck to get to success?

If you look at the word "success," the first three letters are s-u-c – "suck."

You must go through the "suck" to get to success! You have to go through the reps and the grunt work because success doesn't happen overnight.

Success is a journey, not a destination. You can't just start something and boom, you're successful at it!

Everyone talks about Jeff Bezos and his success, but few realize there were 20 years of major, massive debt before he got to his "overnight success" with Amazon.

Success takes a while, and it requires repetition.

Look at Kobe Bryant and Michael Jordan and all the success they had – making shots over and over again.

And guys like Tiger Woods. How many clubs would he use and shots would he take over and over again to get to his level of success?

I could go on and on, but it's not just about sports and the physical aspect of things.

In martial arts, I got my butt kicked a bunch. My nose was busted, my eyebrows split, and I got stitches everywhere. It reached the point where I would get the stitches in the ER but would take them out myself later. I don't recommend doing that, but that's what I did.

You have to go through that not-so-glamorous, drudgery stuff. The repetition. If you're in sales, you must experience rejections and those who say "no." You have to grind out the calls and the emails.

But it's all going to be okay. Just trust the process. Keep steady. Keep going. Ensure you have someone mentoring or coaching you, so you're not just knocking your head against the wall, hoping something good sticks.

Contrary to popular opinion, success is not overnight. But if you do the work, you're going to be successful.

Let Go of the Railing – It Will Be Okay

If you're struggling or challenged with something, just let it go. It's going to be okay. Sometimes the things we hold on to are things we just need to let go of.

It has happened to me in so many different ways. When you are concerned about stuff or are afraid of losing something, let things go, and it will work out. The Universe/God/higher power will take care of things for you.

As my friend, Fenton Joseph, says, "You just got to let go. Let go of the rail. It will be okay." Whatever your challenges or struggles are, understand that it will be okay. I've heard it said this way, "Suicide is a permanent solution to a temporary problem." All the challenges we deal with are temporary. Time can heal everything as long as you have faith – that's the most important piece of it.

Have a good outlook on life. Be optimistic. Believe good things are coming because I believe they are. I am a man of faith and truly believe we are all destined for greatness.

Off with the Old and On with the New

I had a conversation with a young man who I'm blessed to be mentoring, and he is experiencing some challenges as I have over the years.

Our self-concept from the past can hold us back from being the successful person we are destined to become. Some of these "old habits" or not-success-oriented actions could include bad associations or activities and drugs or alcohol – things we don't feel good about. We look at ourselves, judge ourselves, and maybe ask, "How can I be successful?" but we continue to drag all these bad habits with us.

You must rid yourself of your old habits and believe you're a brand-new person today. Take that old self and bury it.

There's a punishment (I don't remember if it was from medieval or ancient times), where if someone committed the crime of murder, the body of the person that was murdered would be attached to the killer, who would have to walk around with the corpse on their back. As the deceased person's skin decayed, the killer's skin would also. Horrible experience!

Many of us are walking around, trying to navigate life and succeed with a "dead person" on our backs! So, I'm encouraging you to rid yourself of that. Believe that you can draw a line, as I like to say, in concrete instead of in the sand. Sand is temporary, but concrete is permanent.

As a kid, I was picked on, bullied, and nicknamed "Spaz." I was uncoordinated and awkward, and whenever I was outside with my friends (well, I don't know if they really were "friends" – more like the people I associated with), they would call me "Spaz." When I went to camp, none of the other campers knew the "old" Steve, so I was able to reinvent myself completely.

You can reinvent yourself anytime! It may require changing some of your associations, but a lot of it is a mind game. You need to convince yourself that you're not that old person. You're a brand-new person! Have a visualization of who you want to become and who you want to be. Take that old self, that old baggage, and bury it. Become a new person instead!

Choose someone you want to emulate. Remember, you'll be a second-class someone else but a first-class you! Take inventory and write down who and what you want to become. Leverage some of your best assets. I don't tend to be super funny or super bold. While I admire those characteristics, I know I have other strengths and qualities.

List your strengths. If you really embrace this, success is imminent. With the right actions, you can continue to grow and build yourself up. Success can be yours with the right knowledge and people surrounding you. But if you hold on to that old baggage, that "dead person," it will be hard to break away from everything negative you don't like about yourself.

Figure out who and what you want to be and surround yourself with people that will uplift and encourage you to become a new person. Today is a new day… draw a line in the concrete!

Get a Routine, Have an Extraordinary Life

I listened to an incredible book with a great message on Audible titled "The 5AM Club: Own Your Morning. Elevate Your Life." by Robin Sharma. Sometimes the day seems to get away from us, and we still have things on our to-do list to get done. We know we should be listening to podcasts, reading, working out, eating right – whatever it happens to be.

Often, when the alarm goes off first thing in the morning, we hit snooze. Before I listened to the book, I started a morning routine, and the book reinforced my decision and sustained me. It's been an incredible part of the peace and productivity I have now. I haven't arrived yet, but the success I'm starting to see today is part of that ritual.

Full disclosure – it's not 5 am for me, and I don't know if it will ever be – it's 6 am. I get up at 6 am every day. My body wakes up (I don't need an alarm typically). I start with my spiritual beliefs of praying. I fix a healthy breakfast (which includes a protein pancake, fruit, and egg whites) plus coffee. I listen to my audiobook while fixing breakfast, giving me typically 20-25 minutes to listen to a book. With Audible, I can get through an average of two to three books per month. Being a learning-disabled, dyslexic guy, getting through two or three books is pretty incredible.

While stretching, I have a self-talk that I go through. Afterward, weather permitting, I go outside and do some spiritual reading. Then, I put on music and do a creative visualization or meditation, and I have a story that I play in my brain. Finally, I journal, listing three things I'm grateful for, send gratitude messages to people, and say additional prayers.

My routine is roughly about 1½ hours long. It's great! It is centering, and it "brackets my day" (from the book "Compound Effect" by Darren

Hardy). This is a way to start and end your day. It's difficult to control everything in the middle, but you can at the beginning and end. It requires getting up early – whether it's 5 am or 6 am (choose what works best for you).

Establishing this morning routine has been tremendous for me. I recommend the book and recommend you start your own routine. And just so you know – I didn't start my morning practice all at once. I added pieces to it. "Atomic Habits" by James Clear talks about habit-stacking. So, I stacked. I did one, added another, and eventually had an incredible morning routine.

Establish a healthy morning routine to wake up early and do healthy activities for your mind, body, soul, and spirit. Start a routine by doing a little and use habit-stacking to build on it. Over time, it will change your life, perspective, and mind, giving you peace and allowing you to live an extraordinary life.

Face Your Dragons and Slay Them Daily

When we say *face your dragons and slay them every day,* we're talking about your fears and obstacles in our lives that stand in our way. And honestly, the more we think about them, the bigger they get.

"The 5AM Club" by Robin Sharma is about routines and building habits by establishing daily routines. What do you do to face your fears daily? If you are not challenging yourself regularly, you're not growing. I work out almost every day, trying to push myself. Those who work out know you must break down muscle to grow muscle. The compound effect of doing things regularly will give you that slight edge that will allow you to grow.

The biggest area that I found to be effective is by conquering the fear that I had. In my martial arts days, I was up against a guy who wanted to kill me. He hated guys who looked like me. He was super strong and aggressive. I had this fear of death going up against him. It was tough, but I confronted my fear and worked through it. I did not avoid it, and obviously, he didn't kill me.

But what is FEAR? False Evidence Appearing Real, and it is worse in our minds than it is in reality.

Competing against him was a great lesson for me and a metaphor for things in life. Everyone has their dragons, things we fear that seem bigger than life. My advice is to do something every day to conquer that fear. For me, public speaking was terrifying. As a kid, I would stutter when asked to read something from a book during class. It was terrifying because I had this learning disability, although I didn't know it then. But I got over it.

My message is this: face those dragons, face those fears, and slay them daily. If you're not challenging yourself daily, you won't grow. Working on your daily goals will transform your life, and you will never be the same.

You Got a Case of the Shoulda, Woulda, Couldas?

Let's talk about taking the limits off! No more "shoulda, woulda, coulda"! Stop the nonsense!

Too many people compare themselves to others on social media, the big screen, TV, movies, or sports figures. Enough already! Don't play the comparison game!

In "Chasing Excellence" by Ben Bergeron, he shares how racehorses don't compare themselves to the other racehorses around them; they do what they do with excellence! According to some scientists, bumble bees should not be able to fly because they have large bodies with tiny wings that are not aerodynamic–yet they fly. Evidently, they don't know they aren't supposed to – they just do what they do.

Focus on the "why" and the "who" – not the "how" and the "what." Focus on where you are going – your "why." Find and surround yourself with people who will uplift and encourage you. Ask yourself, "Do the people I surround myself with have the success and the lifestyle I want?" And the next question is, "Will they invest their time helping me get there?" If the answer is "no" to either question, it's time to find a new "who" in your life.

So, here's the main point: know you are great and made for greatness! If I could succeed with all my life challenges, you can too! Your past and your present don't define you, and other people growing and thriving shouldn't do anything to discourage you. If anything, it should uplift and encourage you!

Whatever is going on in your life, there's a solution. There's a way. Find people in your life who will help you. Focus on the "who" and the "why" and believe there are seeds of greatness inside you!

You can do it!

Do You Rationalize or Is It Rational-Lies?

Do you tend to rationalize, or is it really rational lies? What am I talking about? Many times, we tend to make excuses and rationalize things. We want to justify ourselves for something we're not doing and justify stuff we know we should do better.

Whatever it is – I've been there. Trust me! So, I want to challenge you. I want to tell you that the things you are rationalizing are really just rational lies. They're things that are telling you, convincing you, to stay mediocre. I believe we are destined for excellence, designed for greatness. Don't believe the hype. Don't listen to the lies. Don't accept yourself in saying those lies.

You want to make sure you are speaking the truth and the future. Convince yourself what you are capable of and what you can achieve. Don't rationalize what you think you're not capable of. Know that you can accomplish great things! You have all that it takes. You have the seeds of greatness within you!

So don't tell yourself lies about what you can't do, but the truth of what you can do! Let's stop with the excuses that are making us mediocre. One of my mentors says an excuse is "a skin of a lie stuffed with a reason!" No more excuses!

The truth is you can do it because you are destined for greatness! Stop the rational lies and tell yourself the truth – you are a champion!

What's Your Over and Under?

What's your over and under? I'm not talking about betting or gambling; I'm talking about this: Do you overthink and underwork?

I can tell you that I was very much in that camp for a long, long time. I was the guy who was overthinking everything. Complete analysis paralysis, detail-itus, information constipation – you name it, I was overthinking all of it! Many people want success, want to grow, and want to have a better life, but they are often underworking and overthinking.

I had to make some strong decisions. First, I realized through some amazing mentors that leaders are decisive. They make decisions, and they're not wishy-washy. They see something – they go for it. Of course, they do their due diligence but don't overthink it. They're not afraid to work.

Second, the ones who succeed outwork everyone. Look at the Kobe Bryants and the Michael Jordans of the world. Underworking is definitely not going to get you there. There's hard work, and there's smart-hard work. Take inventory, have a great mindset, surround yourself with amazing people, and stay steady. Do the work, and you will see achievement and success.

When Life Punches You, Punch It Back!

This is the definition of grit: When life punches you in the face, you punch it right back. Don't be a victim, be a victor! When the challenges of life hit you, don't whimper away. Face them head-on.

I saw a great movie, "American Underdog," which tells the true, inspirational story of Kurt Warner. He was pursuing his dream, and life hit him hard. It's a crazy story. Watch the movie, and you'll see what I'm talking about.

Some amazing quotes are included in the movie, such as "Stay in the pocket." You don't avoid challenges and struggles; you stay in the pocket. In other words, when the quarterback is about to throw, and the defense is coming at him, he has to stay right in that little area where he started. He doesn't run away. So, apply that to life. Don't avoid challenges; face them. Put all your challenges in front of you and just punch them.

Also from the movie: "Destiny belongs to the underdog." I have been the underdog my whole life, which motivated me even more than the average person to succeed. So, bring on the opposition -- I am ready! Put me in, coach; I'm ready to play!

Don't avoid the challenges. Fight! Don't give in, and never give up! Be the underdog!

Better by Chance or with Change?

Your life doesn't get better by chance. It gets better with change!

You don't have to be great to get started. You get started to be great! Just start, and as you accomplish something, you become the person you need to be.

I have seen that myself big time. We want success to happen, but it doesn't just happen. If you want your life to change, you have to change. My mom says, "If nothing changes, nothing changes."

So, what are we talking about in terms of change? Change is within us. I'm a huge believer in self-development and personal growth, and I've become an avid reader/audible listener. A phenomenal book, "Ditch the Pitch," by Steve Yastrow, talks about how it starts with you. Change starts from within us, and you must start the process. In the doing, in what you're working through and overcoming, in failing forward, you're going to get great. Everything is hard before it's easy.

So be adaptable, and be willing to change. Be the best version you can be by continually working on improving yourself. Know you're great, but realize you can be greater. Never look for perfection – always look for progress! Never try to be perfect; instead, always work towards excellence. Be the best you can be!

Opinion or Mentorship – What's the Difference?

It's interesting. As my friend says, "Opinions are like belly buttons. Everyone has one." There are many people out there who like to share their opinions. To me, opinions are random and unsolicited. Mentorship is truly deeply rooted. It comes from somebody who's been there, done that, and they have a perspective that you can learn from.

Many great people in the social media world give advice. But that's what it is – advice. It's advice because it can't be mentorship if they don't really know you. I have someone in my life who is an incredible mentor to me. He knows me, and he knows my weaknesses, my strengths, and my situation. He probably knows more about me than almost anyone else in my life – good or bad!

Mentorship allows you to accept advice. We have people in our lives who know us, too –family members, parents, teachers, and coaches. But you need to figure out if they have the fruit on the tree. Is this someone who has succeeded in the arena you want to enter?

When I was looking into the martial arts, I didn't want to take advice from somebody who had tried the martial arts and failed at it. Or someone who never did it but gave advice – how dumb would that be? The internet didn't exist when I started, and I might not have tried it after reading some negative blogs. So you really need to look at who is giving you advice or words of mentorship.

I like using the app "Waze" because I'm a big GPS guy. There are times, however, when I'm a little stubborn. I don't turn on the GPS, and it ends up being a longer trip than I want. GPS tells me to get off four exits earlier than my usual route, but when I don't listen, I end up stuck in traffic for an hour. It's happened to me in mentorship, too. I don't have to listen to my mentor because he's not the boss of me. But when I don't, I'm stuck in traffic for a year – if you know what I mean. A mentor really has perspective allowing them to see the traffic jams and the roadblocks far ahead.

I also look at people who are successful or have hit major milestones. For example, professional athletes who have reached that level did so because they listened to the coach or a mentor – not the fans or the critics. I hear this a lot: "Success is not statistical." You don't survey all the people around you and do what they do. I guess you could if you want to live like everyone else, but not if you want to live like no one else lives. I've also heard, "Observe what the masses do and then do the opposite." Or at least do the same thing as others with the lifestyle you're looking for.

Be very conscious of who's giving you advice in your life. There's an interesting story about crabs in a bucket. If you put a single crab in a bucket, it will get out. But if several crabs are in the bucket, they will all claw the one trying to get out to hold it down. Also, consider that an eagle teaches an eaglet to fly by kicking it out of the nest. In that 10,000-foot free fall, it has to learn how to fly, or it won't be able to protect or feed itself. You can't help someone by protecting them; you hurt them by weakening them.

So let's be conscious of who is giving us advice and determine if it's true mentorship. Mentorship is the biggest game changer in my life. Hopefully, you have someone in your life who is mentoring you, and you're paying it forward like I try to do.

Go Get It!

Procrastination! One of my favorite books is "The Magic of Thinking Big." The author, David J. Schwartz, talks about "success diseases" – detail-itis and procrastination, and those two specifically prevent many people from getting it done.

So, here's a message for you: Just get it done! Stop procrastinating! Stop focusing on all of the details. If you have something that needs to get done, do it! Don't think about it; just do it. It doesn't have to be perfect.

Focus less on the thinking and more on the doing. Especially those of us who have done things and practiced – we're good. Don't overthink it – just do! In the doing, you'll learn and be able to analyze later and correct – and then do it again.

So, go get it! Attack it! Crush it! Don't wait!

Be Here and Now – Trust Your Gut

Success is really a head game. I read a great book called "Can't Hurt Me" by David Goggins. In the book, he talks about how getting hurt is not just physical; in many cases, it's way more mental than physical.

I realized that we often overthink things, getting into our heads too much. Before I got into martial arts, I was huge into tennis. I was the second single tennis player on my high school team. I played tennis seven days a week, 4-8 hours per day. I would play against people not on my level skill-wise, but I would choke in what should have been an easy match. It was frustrating, but I dealt with it.

Eventually, I moved into a new phase of my life, got into the martial arts (years ago), and started training. Martial arts is a Zen Buddhist philosophy. I didn't convert to Zen Buddhism (nothing wrong with it), but I appreciate the different aspects of that particular practice. It focuses on being here and now.

In the martial arts, it is called a "moving Zen." When you hear "Zen," you typically think about people meditating, sitting still. But in the martial arts, when you're in a Zen state, you're moving. I got into that state and was fascinated by the culture and the mindset – just living and being in the now. I went headfirst into it and became very good at clearing my mind, not thinking about anything.

About a year later, I returned to the tennis courts, and interestingly enough, I beat people who were at least on my level without choking. I was able to be in the "now" – in the moment. Some of the best performances in athletics are because athletes can be in the "here and now" and not overthink things.

Whether in business or sales, we tend to be in our heads too much and overthink things. In this experience, I learned to trust my gut and instincts. Be here. Be now. Learn how to focus on being here.

I do a pretty extensive morning practice that includes meditation, prayer, and reading. Try to clear your mind. Focus on what you are doing, and you'll be much more productive. When you get in your head, things can go awry. I believe there are evil forces and good forces. Whether spiritual or religious, there is good, bad, God, and the devil. When we let those evil forces get into our heads, they tear us down.

So stay in the moment. Stay in the "now," and you'll find you'll be much more successful whatever you do.

Stay Consistent, No Matter What

I believe in commitment, consistency, and focusing on the consistency of the message and the effort. It can be anything – LinkedIn, sales effort, networking effort, or work ethic.

A phenomenal book that I read is "Pound the Stone" by Joshua Medcalf. The metaphor is that there were these master craftsmen who were trying to split some really precious stone. They hit it multiple times, and then, finally, it split. The question is: Was it just that one hit that made it split? No, it was multiple pounds on it. So we have to pound the stones sometimes and keep pounding.

It's important to keep going in whatever you start. Don't let life's distractions get in your way. Don't give yourself excuses. Don't quit. Be consistent. Don't let yourself off the hook.

That is what I've tried to live by. I remember that in the martial arts, we'd be "dying" in the heat. Our sensei would "kill" us, but we felt great about it once we got through it.

It's important to keep persevering. Whatever the challenge or struggle is, just keep pushing through. There will be a good result, especially if you're doing the right stuff.

Your Attitude Will Determine Your Altitude

Your attitude will determine your altitude. It's not what happens to you; it's how you react to it that will determine your future.

I don't know what challenges you're going through – financially, spiritually, work, whatever it happens to be – remember that attitude is a decision. You make a decision today when you wake up as to how you want to make the day. My friend and mentor says, "You wake up in action mode. Wake up with the right attitude."

Move forward, and don't dwell on where you are but where you're going. We all have challenges. It's how you react to them.

It's Not What Happens to You; It's How You React to It and What You Learn from It

When I had COVID, it was the worst two weeks of my entire life, but a couple of positive things came from it. One – I lost 11 pounds! I had been trying to lose some weight, and I did. Two – it gave me some major downtime to unwind. My mom often talked about how when your body shuts down, it's God, the universe, or a higher power saying, "It's time just to chill. Your body needs to reset."

I had quite a lot of downtime, which allowed me to unplug from social media. Sometimes we get a little too involved, so I appreciated the opportunity to look at things fresh and focus on what I have in front of me. I wouldn't wish COVID on my worst enemy. It was a crazy two weeks. I was probably a little cavalier about COVID, but it's serious. It hit me really hard.

My dad passed away after having Alzheimer's for at least 15 years, and I remember seeing what death looked like on his face during my visits at the end of his life. About a week into having COVID, I saw death on my face...It was crazy! The good news is that I recovered! So instead of dwelling on the crazy health challenge that I went through, I'm looking at what I learned from it and the benefits I got from it.

It's not about what happens to you but how you react. Sometimes you need to have self-compassion. When I was sick, I had to have a lot of self-compassion for myself because a part of me wanted to go–go–go and always achieve, and I had to allow myself the grace to not be in that mode.

May this be a message of encouragement. We all have stuff that happens to us – whether it's illness-related, job-related, business-related, or relationship-related – there's all sorts of stuff we're going to be dealing with. It's not what happens to you. It's how you react that matters and what you learn from it.

I've heard it said many times by one of my mentors, "We're either winning or learning." Not winning or losing, but winning or learning. This was an opportunity for me to learn, reset, and return stronger than ever.

You Can't Chop a Tree Down with a Butter Knife

You need the right tools to succeed. While a butter knife is a cutting instrument, it isn't as effective as using an ax or saw to cut a tree down.

For many years, I lived by "If it's to be, it's up to me." But what happens if something happens to you like it did to me? As I've learned in life, especially coming back from COVID hell, I have a fresh perspective and a new appreciation for life and growth!

I heard a story about a young man watching a tree-chopping contest. The contestants were using axes to chop trees down. From a distance, he saw one guy who appeared lazy. He would watch the guy chop the tree, take a break, then chop some more. He saw another guy going at it like crazy and assumed that guy would win the contest. He was surprised that the winner was the "lazy" one. He learned the guy would chop and then spend time sharpening his ax, then chop some more. Then he repeated that process.

We need to take opportunities to sharpen our axes, take a break and sharpen our skills -- whether reading a book, listening to a podcast, or sitting at the feet of someone successful, such as a mentor. Whatever it happens to be, we need to take the time to refresh and build ourselves up. I've heard this: We are either tomatoes that are ripening or tomatoes that are dying or rotting. I want to be the kind of guy who is constantly growing and learning.

Keep yourself fresh, making sure you're staying on the cutting edge. We need to grow ourselves personally, professionally, and spiritually. Read/listen to books, listen to podcasts, and associate with people who are where you want to be in life. Avoid toxic people. Make sure you're growing you.

Have the right people around you. I would say this, "If I'm the smartest guy in the room, I'm in the wrong room." I want to be around people who will stretch me and allow me to grow. It's learning to always be better so that you're not a butter knife trying to chop a tree down. It doesn't work! An ax or a knife are both devices that cut – but one is more effective than the other.

You're amazing. You're great. Be conscious of what you're putting in your brain. Surround yourself with the right people that will stretch you and inspire you.

Are These "Diseases"
Preventing You from Succeeding?

Are any of these "diseases" preventing you from succeeding? I'm not talking about medical diseases; I'm talking about three "success diseases" that can stop you. I learned these from reading an incredible book called "The Magic of Thinking Big" by David J. Schwartz.

The three diseases are procrastination, detail-itis, and excuse-itis. I'm speaking to you, but I'm also talking to myself. These diseases have afflicted me for years.

Procrastination

I heard about a cure for procrastination that has helped me tremendously, so I recommend it to anyone suffering from these diseases, especially procrastination. And it's this: hang signs everywhere saying, "Do it now!" If you have something to do, do it now! Doing it now is much easier than waiting because it wears on you. Post that phrase everywhere and make it a habit!

Detail-itis

Detail-itis is the need to know all the details before you start. You don't need to know everything to move forward. That's referred to as "paralysis by analysis." For example, before you get married – do you need to know all the details of what it will be like to be married? You want to know about the person, but the experience? Don't worry about all the details. They'll work themselves out. I'm not saying be irresponsible. You have to do minimal research but don't get crazy about it. Trust me – I was there.

Excuse-itis

Last is excuse-itis. I'm too old. I'm too young. I'm too tall. I'm too short. I'm too this. I'm too that. I've been all that! Never feel like you're too old. I've heard stories about a lady who became a lawyer at age 81. Why wait? Don't make excuses! "Excuse is the skin of a lie stuffed with a reason." So, stop making excuses! You are good enough exactly as you are now!

Let's get rid of these diseases. There is no medicine or supplement to cure them; you have to decide to do it!

Practice Makes Permanent

Practice makes permanent, not perfect. I often get told, "You're so good at what you do." That's because I practice. I found the right way to do stuff, and I have a coach and a mentor to help me do that and perfect it. If you do the wrong thing too many times, it won't help you succeed. For example, Tiger Woods learned to golf correctly, and over time he became successful. But if you're doing the wrong stroke over time, it won't make things better.

Practice does not make perfect; it makes it permanent. So, whatever you're doing, know it will be permanent and difficult to change.

The better you get at something, the more confident you will be. More confidence leads to conviction. And that conviction will bring you success. That conviction, that boldness, that confidence will come through practice.

So, make sure you're practicing your craft properly. Don't wing it. Get really good at it, and then do it over and over again.

Competence will lead to confidence, and confidence will lead to conviction. Once you have conviction, you are unstoppable.

Pillar #2 – Others Focused
and Paying it Forward

Introduction by Oakland McCulloch

Successful people, no matter their profession, have learned and continue to learn from life lessons. None of us are perfect, even though I keep trying to convince my wife I am. We will all make mistakes or fail to accomplish something we set out to do. When that happens, successful people figure out what went wrong and adjust how they do things to ensure it does not happen again.

Anyone who is successful can tell you the principles they live by that allow them to be successful. I have three principles: self-discipline, the desire to be the best at whatever I do, and tenacity.

One thing I remember my father teaching me at a young age was the need for self-discipline. He made sure I knew the difference between discipline and self-discipline and the importance of the latter. He used to tell me, "Son, discipline yourself so others don't have to." Successful people do not need anyone to check up on them to ensure they do the right thing. They do the right thing because it is the right thing to do, even if no one will ever know. That is self-discipline.

Growing up, my father had what he called the 75% rule. I have always lived by that 75% rule. My father used to say, "If you can't do things better than 75% of the people doing it, then you need to do one of two things. Either you need to figure out how to get better at it or figure out something else to do." If you don't want to be the best at whatever you do, I don't want you on my team because I want to win. I don't care if I am playing Old Maid with my 8-year-old granddaughter; I want to win!

Successful people do not accept defeat. They keep at it until they figure it out. One of my heroes, Lieutenant General Hal Moore, used to say, "Life is not like baseball. It is not three strikes and you are out. You just keep trying something new." If you try one thing that does not work, try something else. Keep doing that until you figure out what works. That is what successful people do.

Everyone has their own principles they follow to help them be successful. Steve clearly understands what it takes to be successful, and I have no doubt you will learn from his principles.

—LTC Oakland McCulloch

Pillar #2 Introduction – Being Others Focused and Paying It Forward

For years I was very much closed up. I was so hurt that I protected myself by not connecting with others. I stayed busy – that was my way of keeping people at bay. It was my way of protecting myself and not letting people get in. But doing that was not helping me, and it made me weak. My connections with people were non-existent.

For years my mentor told me, "I don't know what it is about you, but there's something I can't put my finger on." And what it was – I didn't know how to connect. I was just so blocked off. I like to tell the story that for years, I'd sit in front of the TV and watch while eating a whole pint of butter pecan ice cream. I did this three or four times a week. I put on a lot of weight. It felt good when I did it, but afterward, I felt horrible.

That was being closed off, keeping to myself, and not being connected to people. While it felt comfortable at the time, it wasn't good in the long term. It's like working out – after you do it, you feel great, but you have to push yourself to get there. When I found myself reaching out to connect with other people, it felt really good. I felt better. I noticed people reacting positively, and they were appreciative. The more I was "others focused" and connected, the better I felt about myself.

I read "The Go-Giver" by Bob Burg and John David Mann, and reading that book helped and validated much of that. I learned that when you focus on others, your life will also improve. I learned that when you serve others, you become free.

As Zig Ziglar says, "If you want to succeed in life, help enough people to get what they want, and eventually, you'll get what you want. That's what I've done, and hopefully, in this section, these stories and parables will impact you and show you how you can go from inward-focused and self-focused to being a go-giver, someone who pays it forward and gives to others. Be less self-absorbed like I was for many, many years.

Enjoy!

Uplifting and Elevating Others

You make the choice to build up or tear someone else down.

Even though there are so many dark things in this world, we need to be a light. We need to be the ones who uplift others and really elevate them. Don't try to make "your building" bigger by tearing someone else's down. That's not how to do it.

Instead, lift people up! Tell them they can do it!

You can do anything if you put your mind to it! When you have the right people supporting and encouraging you, it's amazing what you can accomplish!

Choose to be around people looking to uplift you – and then be sure to pay it forward. Be a Go-Giver! Be that person who is always looking to serve and help others. If you do this, you will be absolutely blessed! No doubt about it!

For me, the last couple of years has been incredible. I attribute that to taking my eyes off of myself, looking past my hang-ups, and focusing on other people by figuring out how to be a blessing to them.

If you focus on how to help others, I think you'll be surprised at how incredible your life can be! So make sure to be the light! Be the one who uplifts others!

What Does It Mean to be a Go-Giver

I've learned the importance of being a giver in life – how to focus on helping others. I've learned that you will eventually get if you give.

Many times, unfortunately, people have the wrong perspective. They say, "You give me the fire, and I'll give you the wood." No – you need to go to the fireplace and say, "You give me the wood, and I'll help you make the fire."

You can't expect the land to give you a crop without sowing the seed, fertilizing, and cultivating it. You have to plant to eventually reap. We know those are universal laws that apply in life too.

I have found that when I give and help others, I feel better. I feel better about myself and life, and like I am doing something good. When I was "take-minded," self-focused and me-focused, it felt okay but didn't feel great.

For example, if you're in the networking world, you can give by helping people connect with others without expecting something in return. You don't give a referral saying, "Okay. I gave you a referral. Where's mine?" It doesn't work that way.

Find joy in giving! Don't give with the expectation of getting back. Think about when you give someone a gift and their eyes light up, excited. That's what giving is about. You give, wanting the person receiving the gift to find joy.

So make sure you're giving, and then you'll get. Be a Go-Giver!

Excellence with Grace

I have some pretty high standards, as do many of the people I keep in my circle. We are not looking for perfection but for excellence and high standards in every area of our work.

This is important, but I do want to say that what I try to live by and encourage you to live by as well is to have some grace. We are humans, and we are fallible. While I'm working on this daily to improve, I definitely have weaknesses. I'm working towards excellence. I'm working towards having high standards, but I'm not perfect.

If you've heard some of my stories, you know people skills are not my strong suit. I've had to work hard and continue to work hard on my people skills. I've read several books and have read "How to Win Friends and Influence People" by Dale Carnegie many times. My mentor in life says I should read it at least once per year.

People skills are just not in my DNA. I was a second single tennis player, and I did chess and then martial arts, but never team sports. So working with other people is challenging for me. I chose a career at first where I didn't have to have much interaction with people.

While it may not be my strong suit, I work hard at it. I am very driven and focused, and sometimes I get a little edgy. I'm working on it, so I hope those interacting with me will give me some grace. And I encourage you to have some grace with other people.

I've had people that scheduled a connect call with me cancel the call, but that's okay. I'm going to give them a little grace. Depending on how they respond, I'll probably give someone two or three chances. I've been given a lot of second chances, so I will give people grace to redeem themselves.

Yes, we want to be respectful of people and their time, but we need to remember that people will have bad days and stuff going on.

I will tell you that if you're working with people and have a challenge with somebody, talk to them. Go to them with an open spirit. Do not go to them with an angry spirit because that just puts up walls for people.

I'll admit I'm still growing at this. I'm not perfect, but I'm learning, and that's the key here. We are either a tomato that is ripening or rotting, and we want to be people who are growing and learning every day.

Great Gift Suggestions –
The Gift That Keeps on Giving

A lot has been said about gift-giving. I want you to consider giving the gift of you!

The best gift is the gift of self-improvement. Consider giving someone a self-development book or treating them to a conference they have expressed an interest in attending. Or reach out and see how you can be a blessing to them.

One of the best investments you can make is in yourself. Another great investment is investing in others. When considering a holiday or birthday gift, sure, a sweater is nice. But instead, think about ways to help that person be the best version of themselves. Uplift them! Tell them they are amazing! Be an encourager! When you do, you will see the joy it brings to them and to yourself!

So, as you're searching for the perfect gift, think about how you could really bless them – how to help them be the best version of themselves they could possibly be.

Have an Attitude of Gratitude

I have a lot of things to be grateful for, from the Higher Power in my life, to my family, to a great life, a great living situation, profession, and business opportunities. Everything is great in my life! Is it perfect? No, but I'm grateful!

Think about this: whatever you're endeavoring to do – whether it be sales, business, or a profession– it's very easy to get caught up in the drudgery of it. But put in your head space the idea that you're grateful. Be grateful to be doing whatever you're doing—whether you have a great product or service or feel like you are adding value by connecting the dots for people.

Be grateful. Keep the spirit of gratitude inside you when making calls or reaching out by email or messaging. It will come across.

#1 – You'll be more excited to do it.

#2 – You'll find that the essence of the message will be better.

I believe you'll connect better with people, and they'll understand that your motives will perhaps add value to them instead of what you can get from them.

It's Not What, It's Why and Who

It's not the "what;" it's the "why" and the "who" and then the "what" and the "how."

As a society, we've programmed ourselves to find the "what" first. When you finish college, there is tremendous pressure to discover what you will be passionate about and what job, career, or business direction you should take. Finding something you will be passionate about for 45 years is daunting. It's possible but not likely.

"Why"

I've learned from being around some incredible people in my life that it is not about the "what" and certainly not about the "how" – it's about the "why." Simon Sinek gave a great TED talk (the "Golden Circle") and wrote an amazing book called "Start with Why," which is an incredible resource. We need to figure out what our "why" is and what drives us so that we can figure out how we want to live.

We're on this planet, being productive, making money, and creating income – but the question is: How do we want to live? And how does that lifestyle look?

It's important to have a good purpose and to ask: Why am I making money? Hopefully, to live – but also to know: What is my overall purpose? My overarching purpose is to help make a difference.

And that takes me to the next point. I suggest coming up with a mission statement. I created a personal mission statement, which has been an incredible life-changer. It allows me to really focus on and understand what my purpose is. Everything I do must be fulfilling that purpose.

Your purpose, however, does not have to be directly related to your job. It can be a way to fuel your passion and your purpose.

Ultimately, it's a long-term game. Imagine getting into a beautiful car and driving along on a beautiful winding road with no clue where you're going. Unfortunately, that's the way a lot of people live their lives. They think, "Let me look for this really cool car." First, you need to know the end destination, and then you can figure out what you're going to drive and what road you will take.

"Who"

From the "why," it comes down to the "who," which is often overlooked. I've had some wonderful people – incredible mentors – come into my life who have made all the difference.

In life, you need a GPS, which is the "who" – a mentor to help you. This person is someone to listen to and advise you. So, who are you listening to?

Once you have the "who," you can figure out the "what" and eventually the "how."

Your Purpose

So, what is your ultimate purpose in life? Are your actions pointing you toward your life's purpose, goals, and mission?

What is Effective Communication?

There are many ways to communicate other than through written text, such as video and voice text. A typed-out message is great, but you can miss some stuff in the translation. Written messages don't express emotion like a video or voice text can. And while I know that emojis can be a way to soften things up and add some humor to the message, I am not a big emoji guy. For me, there's something about voice inflection and facial expressions that help get the message across better.

I know there is a time and place for everything. Some people may prefer written text messaging to video or audio, but I think it's much better to communicate through video or voice text/messaging. That is my recommendation. Does it have to be exclusively that? No, of course not.

There are some great apps out there that allow you to connect your email with video. For those trying to get new jobs or land a new client, maybe it's worth putting a video together and sending it to the prospect. When you're communicating, choose the style with which the recipient of your message is more comfortable.

It doesn't mean you can't be you – you should be yourself. You will always be a second-class someone else, so be a first-class you.

Here are some helpful tips. If you're in a business environment dealing with a very detailed and slow-paced person, you might slow down and live in that detailed world.

Have you heard of the DiSC Assessment? If you haven't studied the DiSC personality assessment, I recommend it because it is really good. I'm a big believer in it.

D = driven, decisive, "dominance"

I = inspiring, center of attention, fun, "influence"

S = supportive, people-pleasing to a degree, "steadiness"

C = calculating, cautious, "conscientiousness"

Knowing the different personality styles can help you in communicating. For example, if the person you want to talk to is a "C" and you are an "I," then that person probably won't like it if you're all over the place, excited, and fast-paced, and it could throw that person off in their business environment. Conversely, if you're doing something socially, "Is" are welcome because they make things fun and exciting.

The DiSC assessment is a great way to figure out how to deal with people. I've tried to live in all the quadrants and not focus on only one. If you live in all those quadrants, you can relate to many people. Years ago, a good friend and mentor told me, "You will get paid the most based on being able to relate and attract the most people." So be as relatable and as attractive to others as possible. Think about what's effective and what will work well for people and go that route.

Keep in mind that technology is always changing. How we communicate is changing, so it's never one-and-done. Study the DiSC personality styles and try to live in all quadrants. Try video or voice text sometimes instead of just written text.

Add Value, Lose Nothing, Gain A Lot!

By adding value, you lose nothing and gain a lot! We live in such a self-absorbed world today. Take "selfies." When you see a group picture, do you look to see your face first? We live in a very self-focused world. But I will say this – the more I found myself looking to add value, to build other people up, to edify others, the better it made me feel, as well as those around me. Adding value to others helps to make the world a better place.

Many people out there – and I was one– think they must tear others down to make themselves feel better. But I learned that wasn't true. I've heard it said: "You don't knock down others' buildings to make your building look taller." That is not the way to make yourself better or to make others better.

You want to help people grow and make their buildings better. I've heard, "Stand on the shoulders of giants." If people around me are better because I'm in the room, I've done something great. So, let's always look to add value and build each other up.

I've also heard, "When one candle lights another candle, it doesn't lose anything; it gains more light." I love the idea of being the light, and I believe it's our mission on this planet to be the light. If we can help shine a light, be the light, lift others, and add value to people, what a great world this would be. I know that sounds "Pollyanna," but why not try to add value and uplift people?

I love networking and getting together with people. Sometimes there is skepticism with people asking, "What's the angle?" The angle is that I want to see how I can help you. That's it. I know that if you give, you'll eventually get. Believe me when I say, "You are amazing! You are incredible! You make a difference! Believe that you are special and that the world needs to know who you are and what value you bring to the world!"

So, show it! Not just by showing up but by building others up. That was described to me as "edification," meaning lifting others up, building people up, and always looking to have them feel better about themselves. Leave them better off than when they came to you.

Look for ways to be of value and service to others. Never look to take; always look to give. Eventually, the Law of Reciprocity will kick in — when you give, eventually, you get. As it says in the Good Book, "Press down, shake it together, overflowing." (There's more to this Scripture, but I'll just keep it to that.) You always want to continue adding value to people.

Be a Giver, Not a Taker

We are in a world where people always try to take from us. So, we need to be in a place where we are giving. It's interesting because it seems like people have an agenda.

I connected with a young man, 24 years old, a car sales guy. I suggested we connect over a phone call. He said, "I'm a texter." I responded, "Okay, and you're in car sales?" Then I added, to be funny and make a point, "Hey, I might be interested in getting a Lexus. I'll text you when I need one." And he said, "That would be great." Then I said, "Actually, no thanks because I don't text." He said, "Oh, okay, I could also take a phone call." I said, "I thought you were only a texter."

While this conversation didn't lead anywhere, it's interesting how people can be guarded and skeptical. I don't know why that is.

Be the light instead. Be the one to inspire others. I believe I'm called to inspire people and add value to their lives. When you go out there, and you're networking or connecting, or if you're in sales or any service-oriented organization, be a giver first. It's the law of sowing and reaping – give, and then eventually, you get. You can't go up to a fireplace in the middle of winter and say, "Hey, give me heat, and I'll put in the wood." No, that's not how it works. You have to give and then get.

You've probably heard me speak about farming. You must sow before you can reap a harvest. And it's the same thing with us – we need to remember that we have to give. Be a giver, not a taker; eventually, good will come to you. It's the Law of Reciprocity, and it's bound to happen.

Have You Walked in Their Shoes?

Have you walked in their shoes? Are you judging or putting down people, looking down on them? Here's some friendly advice: Until you've walked in their shoes, try not to judge. I'm not perfect at this; I'm still working on it.

Ask yourself this: If you walked in their shoes for their entire life, would you feel the same about them as you do now? I read a story in "7 Habits of Highly Effective People" by Stephen R. Covey. He talks about a man on the subway in New York City. It's calm until a father with two kids gets on, and suddenly, it's mayhem with the kids all over, jumping, screaming, and yelling. The man is looking down. The man can tell the father is in a fog, oblivious. Initially, the man tried to be patient, but he noticed the father not doing much and couldn't help himself by asking, "Sir, do you see what's going on here? Your kids are disrupting. What's going on?" The father turned to him and said, "Yeah, I'm sorry. I don't know what to do. We just came from the hospital. My wife passed away an hour ago." And, of course, the man's judgment went away.

This story illustrates how we look at things through our own lens versus what is happening to others. Be conscious of that before you judge someone else. Try to see what's going on. You don't know what occurred in their life today or earlier on in their life. I thank God I've been given some grace in my life because I've made a lot of mistakes.

So, before we judge people, let's give them the benefit of the doubt. Let's have some grace and compassion for people.

Who, What, Where, When, and Why

When I was in school, we had to do book reports in a who, what, where, when, and why format. It's amazing how much time we invested in that, but I wonder how much time we invest in our life and future. So, I want to try and give it a different spin. It's not a book report – it's your life.

WHO

Who are you spending time with? "Who Not How" by Dan Sullivan is a great book on this subject. Whose voices are you hearing? Are they in line with who you want to be? Be conscious of that.

WHAT

What do you want? What are you willing to give up? What kind of time are you spending? Those are important "whats" to consider when you want to succeed.

WHERE

Where are you spending your time? Where are you looking to go? And in particular, where are you going?

WHEN

The time is now. Do it now! Don't think about tomorrow. At one point in my life, I had stickers posted everywhere saying, "Do it now!" Don't wait – hesitation is devastation.

WHY

This is the most important one. Why are you doing what you do? I love the book, "Start with Why" by Simon Sinek. You've got to know why you're doing something. If you don't know your way, then you really don't know what you're doing. I love to say it like this: If you don't have a final destination, you won't like where you end up. You need to know the destination - the why. Super important!

Take your life seriously. Do your best.

Are You Asking the Right Questions?

I have read "Good Leaders Ask Great Questions" by John C. Maxwell several times. It's a phenomenal book. The last time I read it, it reminded me of the value of asking questions. The #1 people skill is knowing a person's best subject is themselves. When you're having a conversation with someone, don't start talking about yourself. Try to get the other person to talk about themselves by asking questions.

Dig deeper into their answers with follow-up questions to learn more. – don't make it like a checklist. Where are you from? Okay – check. What do you do? Okay – check. Instead, ask follow-up questions such as: Where are you from? Why did you move away from there? Have you moved around a lot? Were you born and raised there? You can go two, three, or four levels deep on every question. And what does that tell them? It shows you genuinely care and you want to know more about them.

If you're looking to attract people, whether in sales, business development, or team building, or maybe you're on the dating scene and trying to find the right person, it's appropriate to connect with people. As the Master Connector, I'm talking about connecting.

So ask questions. Those in business might hear concerns or objections, and I've learned that typically the first objection isn't the real one, so it's important to ask questions to find out. For example, someone says, "I can't afford it." You say, "May I ask you a question – why?" Keep asking "why," – but you need to change it up. Try alternatives such as, "Why is that?" or "Can you tell me why?" Rephrase it a little bit.

If you dig a little deeper, you'll get to the heart of it where typically, you can unpack it and maybe even come up with ways to address those concerns.

Make sure you're asking questions about yourself too. Ask: "What am I looking to accomplish?" and "What am I doing here?" It's so important to be asking the right questions. Not just any questions for the sake of hearing yourself, but the right questions. If you do that, success is imminent.

In Our Weaknesses, There is Power

In our weaknesses, there is power. I know that sounds contradictory, and it is to a degree. I'll be honest with you. For years I tried to hide my weaknesses and the things I felt vulnerable about. But all that did was block people out, preventing me from connecting with them. When I exposed and shared those weaknesses, I noticed people would lean into me.

Sharing my weaknesses provided the power to connect with and build relationships with others. We tend to want to protect ourselves, but I found amazing strength in doing that. I was also able to connect with others, and my confidence grew. That confidence and power somehow magically came from my weaknesses.

So I recommend not being afraid to share some of your vulnerabilities. You don't have to share anything crazy, but sharing some is okay. I finally found peace in who I am and no longer play the "comparison game." I'll always be a second-class someone else, but I'll be a first-class me – and I'll say the same thing to you.

Understand that you are awesome. You are amazing. Don't be afraid to be vulnerable and share your weaknesses. You will be amazed at what power you will get. Not an ego power, but power in confidence!

To Increase Your Self-Worth, Uplift Others

I've had incredible people in my life who have uplifted me, and I've shown that appreciation to them, and I've been blessed to be able to pay it forward. Nothing is better than uplifting somebody else – empowering, helping, and serving them.

I'm not just talking about a quick "Hey. You're awesome." I'm talking about uplifting them, showing that you care and that they have value. As you grow and build them up, you build yourself up.

It feels great to serve and uplift others, especially when you get messages back and voice texts from others to share their appreciation for you. Those really build me up. One of my mentors says, "Your self-esteem and self-worth are not what you think of yourself, but what you think other people think of you." So how do you know that? You don't, but if they start expressing their feelings about you, there's nothing better.

Now, there are other things you need to do to grow your self-worth, but this is one incredible way to do it. Serve others, focus on being a blessing to others, and uplift others. Nobody likes a "Debby Downer" or people who talk negatively.

Make sure your conversations are uplifting another person. Talk about positive things happening in their life, and you'll see how much it will help you with your self-worth.

Pursue Greatness or Mediocrity Will Pursue You

We are all here for a higher purpose or calling. If you don't pursue greatness, then mediocrity will pursue you!

Your calling will be accomplished through something other than your job or business.

I've heard, "Your paycheck doesn't have to be your passion, but it can help find or fund it."

Sometimes your passion or purpose or whatever it is you want to do that is great could be missions work, feeding the homeless, or another cause you want to support. Whatever it is – make sure you're pursuing it.

If you don't pursue it, a life of mediocrity, not a life of greatness, will pursue you.

We want to be better and to have a higher purpose and meaning here on this planet. So go ahead and do it – fulfill your passion. Just remember that it does not have to be through your job or business; it can be done in other ways.

We are all here for a reason, a purpose. For me, it's to touch many people positively, be the light, uplift, and inspire others – to be a beacon of hope and bring people to a better place so they can feel empowered. That's why I do everything I do to fulfill that cause.

Hopefully, you have a purpose. If you don't, surround yourself with people who do. Be inspired by them and seek to discover your own purpose.

You're Here to Accomplish Great Things!

You are here to accomplish great things! Don't let anyone tell you otherwise! You are amazing and can do anything you put your mind to!

If you don't quit, you win!

You have all that it takes. You were born for this moment. You have the seed of greatness inside of you! You are engineered for greatness. You are more than a conqueror through Him who gives you strength!

Don't let anyone steal your dream. You can do anything you want to.

That's the self-talk I have and the self-talk you should have. Every day look yourself in the mirror (the "mirror technique") and say only positive self-talk to yourself.

Don't listen to the voices outside your head or in your head that feed you seeds of doubt… Plant seeds (words) of life and hope! You can do it! You are made for this moment!

Pillar #3 – Connecting Authentically

Introduction by Marques Ogden

For me, authenticity is being open and vulnerable with other people when they ask you for your input. It's about being true to yourself regardless of external influences or pressures around you. It's about showing up in the world as the 100% authentic version of you at any given moment.

I'm so proud of my good friend Steve Spiro for the work he's done to show up as his authentic self in this world. I've worked with him as his coach to help grow his brand, and we've built an incredibly genuine connection. He's the master connector and is the epitome of authenticity. I am honored he asked me to be a part of this amazing book because standing beside a man like Steve is a true honor. Steve and I genuinely align on our passion for being authentic, making authentic connections, and spreading that message of importance to everyone around us.

—Marques Ogden

Pillar #3 Introduction – Be Authentic

Authenticity is extremely important. You've to be authentic. I've learned that people connect with you better if you lead with your weakness and vulnerabilities. I read a book that said you're more relatable when you admit a mistake. People like you better. If you're perfect, people tend not to connect with you.

I love being able to share some of the things I went through—the challenges and insecurities. I won't air all of my dirty laundry, but I will share some of my struggles at some point in the conversation. It's amazing how people open up when you do that. I also like to be authentic and vulnerable on social media, which I do when talking to someone on a coffee meeting or a connect call on Zoom.

It's important always to be your true self– whether in the dark or in public. Be who you are and be authentic. Be real. That's super important!

Hopefully, this section will inspire you on the importance of being real. The younger generation can sniff and smell the lack of authenticity. So, make sure you are authentic.

In our weakness, there is power. You will see the power in connecting with others when you're weak and show your vulnerabilities. I found that the more I was vulnerable and showed weakness, the more I made powerful connections with others, and I had much more confidence.

So lead with those weaknesses. You'll see how life will be better for you!

Are You Being Pushy or Persuasive?

I'll start with a quick story. Growing up, I was shy, introverted, picked on, and bullied. I didn't have many people skills; instead, I had the personality of a brick. After college, I started an advertising company with a partner who had good people skills. He said, "We're going to do something great for you and the company. We're going to send you to a course." The course was Dale Carnegie, and one of his great books, "How to Win Friends and Influence People," has become one of my favorite go-to books.

Once when I was on a call with several people, one individual called out another person in front of the whole group. I know it made this person feel bad. So here are a couple of tips I've learned from Dale Carnegie's book.

Sandwich approach

Dale teaches never to criticize, condemn, or complain. But if you do need to correct someone, timing is everything. If you must address something bothering you or some corrective criticism, do not do it with others present. Take that person off to the side and tell them in private.

One suggestion is to use the "sandwich approach." Start with something positive, then say what's on your mind, and finish with something positive again.

It might sound something like this, "Hey, Joe, you're a great asset here, and I really appreciate your hard work and discipline and [never say "but"] one of the things I'd like to share with you is that I'd like to see you do [this] instead of [that] because when you do [this], it's not serving us very well. You are amazing, and I'm excited to see you thrive in our organization."

It's extremely important to say it this way and not make people feel condemned. Look at it this way: we want to grow our businesses and attract people, not repel them.

In terms of pushy or persuasive, if you're being pushy, you have an agenda. If you tend to get right to the point, try to be a little softer. Yes, we must get our point across, and we are not looking for people to step all over us. But we also must consider the timing, the words we use, and how they are said.

Permission approach

If you find yourself doing these kinds of things, try using another technique called the "permission approach." Ask, "If I saw something that might serve you better, would you like me to tell you about it?" If they say yes, then ask, "Are you sure? It might not be comfortable." Then say what you need to say. Just blurting it out doesn't serve anyone.

Be persuasive but not in a manipulative way. Remember, people do business with people they know, like, and trust. And when we are pushy or agenda-based, it will repel people.

Your Daily Actions Speak Loudly

Being loud and obnoxious is not always the way to get someone's attention, especially if you want to get the "right attention." What resonates with me is what you do every day – in other words, your daily actions.

One of my mentors said, "What you do speaks so loudly that I can't hear what you say."

What kind of message (good or bad) are your daily actions saying?

Me, I'm a head-down, focus-on-the-goal, grind-it-out kind of guy. When I hear the loud noise about people with flash-in-the-pan success, I say quietly in my head, "Okay, great for them, but watch out, world, here I come!"

I'm not doing it for the fame and fortune. I'm doing it to inspire others, to be the light and glorify my Heavenly Father!

What about you?

Leading with a Limp

Many of us are leading in several different ways: in our jobs, in our businesses, on social media, spiritually at a church or a synagogue, at a nonprofit organization, or in our homes. Whatever it is, we are leading in some way.

There is a misconception that to be a leader, you need to be perfect. And I will say straight up that's not true. I can't speak for anyone else but I can speak for myself – I am far from perfect. In fact, I believe some of my challenges are some of the strengths I bring to the table.

When I hear the expression "leading with a limp," it means leading with your weaknesses. It means understanding that you have some weaknesses, but I think those are what make you stronger. They allow you to be vulnerable and to show yourself vulnerable to the people you lead. If you've seen me in person or have seen my videos or live shows, you can tell I'm definitely not perfect.

I'm working on my communication skills. Being shy, bullied, and introverted as a kid put me in a box. I didn't have many relationships growing up. My comfort zone was in my room watching TV. That's where I lived. I didn't interact with my family, let alone friends. To make it worse, I went to a commuter high school and a commuter college, so building relationships was foreign to me. Communicating and relationships are definitely my weakness, but I'm working on those. I'm growing that every day. I read a lot of books on communication. I'm constantly growing to be a better communicator, relationship-builder, and able to lead and help others.

I have also struggled with a learning disability. I'm not a great reader. I have a challenge reading, so I thank God for Audible. I can go through an average of three books a month, which is tremendous. Reading was tortuous for me – it really was. I couldn't retain a lot of it as it was just really hard. When someone sends me a communication, I may not retain it well, so if you've dealt with me, you know that about me. I might completely misread what another person sends me in the form of an email or text, but I'm working on that. I may have to read it four, five, or six times to really understand it instead of understanding it the first time I read it.

John C. Maxwell says, "Leadership is an example." So, we're always an example in one way or another. Just know that you don't have to be perfect. How I live my life is never about perfection, but it's always about striving for excellence. And know you can be a great leader if you lead with your vulnerability, weaknesses, or limp! It's not about perfection. People will appreciate your transparency and relate to you more, and it will help them trust you more.

So that's my message: if you're in a position to lead people, know you're good enough. You're in a good place. Don't try to be perfect, but always strive to be better; always strive for excellence.

Are You a Thermometer or a Thermostat?
Are You an Egg, a Carrot, or a Coffee Bean?

Are you a thermometer or a thermostat?

When you enter a room, do you gauge the temperature and then settle in with that temperature? Or are you a thermostat that changes the temperature?

Open, people are given an environment and just live with it. We have the ability, however, to be an influence. I like to believe when I walk into a room, and I hope you feel the same way, that the room is blessed because I'm here. I don't mean that in an arrogant manner. I believe we all should feel we have value. So make sure you feel that way.

Make sure to bring your energy, excitement, knowledge, gifts, talents, and skills with you when you come into a room. Don't just settle into a room, job, company career, or business. You can change the atmosphere, environment, or culture.

I want to share a story I had heard before, but I heard it again recently, and it impacted me more this time.

When you put an egg into boiling water, what happens? It gets hard because the water influences the structure of the egg.

When you put a raw carrot into boiling water, what happens? It goes in hard but comes out soft.

But what happens when you put a coffee bean into hot water? The flavor and color of the water completely change.

So – will you be like the egg, the carrot, or the coffee bean?

Make a decision to be the coffee bean! You can be the change agent – you really can!

You can change the culture of whatever organization or company culture you are a part of. Be the one who brings on change.

Be the thermostat! Be the coffee bean!

Don't Pitch, Really Connect

When you're on a call, don't pitch! It's ugly and repulsive! Instead, connect with that person. Learn more about them and understand their needs, desires, and challenges.

Tell stories about people who have used your services and how it has benefitted them. The more you connect with people emotionally, the better it will be. People feel pitching is like coming at them with kicks and punches, and it's so much better for you and the other person if you start connecting.

Here's another "secret" I've learned from some incredible people in my life, my mentors. They have taught me to be agreeable. That does not mean you have to say "yes" to everything, but what I've learned is the "feel – felt – found" technique. Use it when you don't necessarily agree with what the person says: "I know how you feel. In your shoes, this is what I felt; let me tell you what I found." Then tell them your opinion, your version, in a respectful tone. Exercise your people skills. Be agreeable and smile. Nod your head as you're talking to them. This helps to create agreement subconsciously and subliminally without forcing your opinion on someone.

Be agreeable. Start connecting. Be understanding of their needs, wants, desires, and challenges. Look at people who successfully connect with others and model what they do.

Seek to Understand Before Being Understood

Do you seek first to understand before being understood? So many times when someone is speaking to us, we just can't wait to talk. When we finally get that opening, we then feel compelled to state our opinion or what we are thinking. Can you relate?

Let's focus on being a better connector. By not truly listening, you can miss what the person is saying. You don't know what they are thinking and where they are coming from unless you seek to understand them.

Some of the most valuable advice from one of my closest friends and mentors is: "Listen twice as much as you speak. Remember, God gave us two ears and one mouth to listen twice as much as we talk." This is especially true when you are around someone with much more success than you, like he is with me. Regardless, it's good people skills.

I challenge you to try it. You may be shocked! Really hearing what that person is saying can help you better understand where they are coming from. The best way is to give them your time, so take a deep breath, listen, and ask questions.

Do that, and you will level up your communication skills.

It's a New Connected Era – But Are We Really?

We talk about how we are in this new connected era – but are we really? So many people want to get "connections" on social media, but are we really connecting? Are we really taking the time to have conversations, to get to know each other?

I love being a networker on LinkedIn and other platforms when I can, but it's not about having a huge connection list. Instead, the point is: who can I connect with next that could be an amazing relationship? Maybe we can collaborate on something that would benefit each of us – something we can do together. I've created some incredible relationships through LinkedIn to jump off the platform itself and have a real conversation, a phone call, or a real Zoom call (or whatever platform you choose for meetings or Teams). You'll be amazed at the meaningful relationships you can establish when you do this.

It's incredible what happens when you really connect – and I mean being able to tell each other stories and engage in real conversations. It may even include being vulnerable. I'm not saying you must share some deep, dark personal stuff, but I suggest opening up. One of my favorite things is leading with my vulnerability and weaknesses. This lets people know, "Hey, I'm human. I'm okay. I'm just a regular guy who would love to hear your story. Tell me your story, and I will tell you mine."

Try to connect deeper than just on a superficial level. Watch barriers come down, and people open up. It will be like the kids inside come together to play. I've seen great partnerships and collaborations form from creating real connections.

We have a vast technology world to take advantage of, but we are not connected if we're not truly getting to know each other. I challenge you to go out there and connect, be the light, uplift, and encourage someone.

Are You Really Connecting?

Are you really connecting with people? It is important to connect with people effectively to succeed in business.

Here are some simple tips for connecting authentically.

1) Smile with your eyes.

For many people, when they smile, it comes across as a little goofy or insincere. So try to smile with your eyes. It means you're approachable, friendly, and warm. Practice smiling with your eyes.

2) Speak in the "third person" instead of giving advice directly.

Try to talk in the third person instead of giving direct advice to people. Many times people want to share their opinion and talk about controversial things. You should avoid controversy, but if you're going to say something critical, talk about it in the third person and talk about yourself. Don't say, "You have this, and you should do this." Instead, say, "You know, in that situation, I've done this...." That's what I mean by speaking in the third person. Tell a story.

3) Compliment them.

Straight out of "How to Win Friends and Influence People" (by Dale Carnegie): people like to be complimented. People want to feel good, so find something to compliment them on. Compliments must be sincere and truthful.

4) Get them talking about themselves.

Super important! Say, "Hey, I'd love to hear about your story, your journey." Get them talking. When I meet somebody out and about and they ask what I do, I might give them like 20 seconds on what I do, and then I go right into asking questions about what they're doing and what they're about. People love to talk about themselves; it's their favorite topic.

I hope these tips help you to start really connecting with people.

Mirror and Matching to Connect More Effectively

An effective way to connect with people on their level is to figure out what they relate to. Granted, how we connect with others has changed. We often don't meet in person; it's on a video platform.

Now, more than ever, we are in the spotlight, and people are looking at us. When we meet in an office or a coffee shop, a lot of activity is happening in the background. But on a video call from your home office, you have no choice but to connect.

I have been blessed with amazing mentors who have taught me a lot. I learned that when connecting with someone, you want to mirror and match their communication style. For example, speed, tempo, and volume. If they are fast-talking, you should speed up your communication during that interaction. If they're speaking slowly, then match their pace. Even if it feels awkward, adjust, at least for that scenario.

Tempo is the pace of the speech. Fast-pace, slow-pace, etc. All of these things are important. We tend to be monotone. It might be good to change it up a little – a little fast and then bring it back a little.

If you want to connect, you must do so on their level. If they speak softly, you need to bring your tone down. If they talk loudly, then bring your tone up.

I've heard people comment that it's tricky with Zoom. If the person you're speaking with crosses their leg with their right foot, you cross your leg with your right foot. If they fold their arms over their chest, you can do the same. But avoid being obvious about it!

Those are visual cues. They might be subliminal, but they are there. People relate more to people who are similar to them. I know there's a lot of talk about inclusion, and I'm all for that. But people relate to people that they feel have similarities to them. We can do that – maybe not culturally or ethnically – but we can have similar communication styles for the moment.

Be conscious of your communication style when interacting with people. You'll be amazed at what will happen and how much more effective at communicating and connecting you can become.

The Importance of Your Personal Brand

I enjoy helping people establish their personal brand on sites like LinkedIn. Many people make their LinkedIn profile read like a glorified resume. That's not what it's for; it conveys who and want you're about.

Creating your LinkedIn Profile

Title (or headline). Look at the title/headline on your profile. It shouldn't be, in my opinion, your job title. Instead, it should be what you're about. If you're like me, it can be multiple things.

About section. What does your about section say about you? Did you include anything personal about yourself? Or is it only a job description of your tasks for your job or career? This should express who you are and what you're about.

Profile photo. Your picture should reflect your personality and not be too goofy or personal because it's a business profile. For example, you don't want to have a picture of you and your dog. Save that picture for other social media platforms (like Snapchat or Instagram).

So many people try to convey what they think people want to see instead of who they really are on social media. This should be your personal brand, not what you're about.

Creating a mission statement

My mentors encouraged me to create a mission statement for many years, and I finally did it. It's been a game-changer for me. Everything in my life has to line up with that mission statement. And if it doesn't, I'm not going to do it. One of my mentors said, "You put a point where you're at right now, and then you put a point where you want to go. Draw a straight line. Anything not taking you where you want to go is a detour."

And where you want to go are your ultimate goals, your mission in life. Is it taking you there? If not, it's probably a distraction. So it's important to pay attention to your personal brand.

Have a Story to Tell

What's your story? Do you have a story to tell? It's important to know your story, understand it, and be able to articulate it.

You need to lead with some of your weaknesses and your vulnerabilities. When I tell my story – a shy, introverted kid from the Bronx – I will joke and put myself down a little. You want to tell a compelling story about who and what you're about, not just what you do. Too many people tell their story leading with what they do, such as, "I'm a financial planner and..." Please! If I may make a suggestion: don't do that! Tell me about yourself.

Tell me about where you were born and raised. Maybe about what your parents did. What influenced you? What were the things that drove you? Perhaps a little bit about your family. All those things are important because people want to do business with people – with you.

Write out your story. Script it out. You don't want to read it, but you'll want to script it out so you can see it. Look at it: Do I need this? Maybe I could change that. Then record it to yourself, not for others to hear. Listen to the recording and make adjustments if needed.

It's essential to get your story down so you can be comfortable telling it when you're having these networking conversations. Know your story and be ready to tell it.

You, Too, Can Be a Master Connector

I didn't start as a master connector. I was shy and introverted by nature – I still am. I was the guy who didn't have many friends. If I was in a group of people, I was listening, observing from the corner, watching. Still, to this day, if I'm in a large group of people, I like to be the guy observing. Being in my comfort zone is dangerous, so I have learned to push myself outside of it.

I make connections with a spirit of openness, not with an agenda. I connect with people with the thought, "How can I add value to you?" I live my life and talk to people on purpose. It's interesting how open people are and how open-spirited they can be. If you perceive people as close-minded, they probably will be because you will project that.

Talk to people when you're out and about in the community. Just say hello, and share a sincere smile. Say something. Maybe comment on something they're wearing. Just have a conversation, not an agenda.

Social media is another excellent way to reach out and connect with people. Please don't ignore someone who reaches out to you. If you are connected with me on social media, you want to connect with me. Why would you want to have a connection but not connect? It makes no sense.

Networking events, whether virtual or in person, are a great way to connect. Being on a Zoom call can make it easier to ask someone to connect with you and schedule a talk. Use the resources available.

However, understand that networking is not to try to solicit or push an agenda onto someone. Networking should be sincere and something you want to do. If you're forcing it, then you probably should walk away. Be open, connect, and you can be a master connector too.

Pillar #4 – Building a Community and Growing Your Connections

You don't meet people by accident. There's always a reason, a lesson or a blessing.

MASTER connector tip

#MasterConnector

Introduction by Jordan Mendoza

Building a community is everything. It takes time, but it is SO worth it.

When I first became active on LinkedIn in 2019, I didn't see the platform as a community-building tool. It was because I didn't understand the platform at that point. It wasn't until I started to create consistent content and engage with my audience that I saw a community being built before my eyes.

You see, engagement sparks engagement. I had been creating content but needed to engage with the people that interacted with it. Everything changed once I made that shift and became focused on engaging and getting to know my audience on a deeper level. Before I knew it, I went from 7,000 to 20,0000 followers and eventually reached LinkedIn's 30,000 connection limit, which helped grow my following.

Fast forward three years later, I have a million plus people viewing my content each quarter and have more than tripled my audience size.

Steve and I connected in 2021, and the first thing I noticed was how good of a connector he was. It didn't feel awkward or sleazy but rather like a friend I've known for a while looking to catch up.

Steve is really great at reading people and finding common ground. I have no doubt that his knowledge and the material in the book will greatly help you on your journey to becoming a Master Connector!

—Jordan Mendoza

Pillar #4 Introduction – Build a Community and Grow Your Connections

Yes, it's a cliché: Your network is your net worth. It is, and it is important to build a community and grow your connections for many reasons.

First, it creates a support system. You have people around you who will support you. As you build a community, you also grow a network, especially if it's on social media like LinkedIn. If you have something you want to platform, some message you want to get out, you can broadcast that message to a large group of people who have agreed to want to know you. So build out that community and look at it as a community, not as numbers.

When I connect with people on LinkedIn, I immediately say, "Let's jump on a call." Not everyone says, "Yes," but I make an attempt. I want to know the people in my community and build relationships. Community is building relationships, not just having 21,000 connections but a network of people who know you and know what you're about. Hopefully, you know a lot of them – or at least attempt to want to know them.

Often, I make referrals and introduce people in my network. The reception is usually positive because I've established credibility and built a community. So continue to grow your connections.

This section will really help you if you're someone like me, where connecting is not part of your instinct. I was a shy, introverted kid, and growing a huge connection list wasn't in my DNA. At the time of this writing, I have 18,000 connections on my phone and close to 22,000 LinkedIn connections, and those numbers will probably increase by the time you read this book. It's crazy! And it's not a number to me; it's about how many people we can connect with, build relationships with, and impact.

The bigger the community, the more impact you have. In my case, positive impact. It's so important to do that. If you're looking for a job, you will want an extensive network, so grow it now before you're in that position. If you want to promote your business, build your network first. Marketing or promoting to a network you've built is much easier. But never market or promote in a way that does not "add value" to your network.

I'm always looking to add value. At the end of every networking call, I ask, "What can I do to be a blessing to you? How can I add value to you?" Or "Can I make a couple of suggestions?" And then, I might recommend a book or suggest they attend a networking meeting I'm a part of, make some introductions, or even have them be a guest on my LinkedIn Live.

Whatever it is, I'm always looking to add value. So make sure you're building your community intending to add value. That will truly be an asset to you. It's not just about the numbers.

Three-Legged Stool of Networking

Even though I grew up a shy and introverted kid from the Bronx, I got into self-development and networking after college. With the help of an incredible mentor, I've become a huge networker. My theme is that there is danger in my comfort zone, and I always try to push myself out of my comfort zone every day.

I want you to understand that if I can network, so can you! Over time, I realized some commonalities with my networking skills and started developing the "Three-Legged Stool of Networking:" traditional, social media, and unconventional.

Traditional

The first leg of the stool is traditional, and it's what you expect – BNI events, chamber events. The key is to make the most of these networking events and understand who your clients are and where they'd like to be.

Many people go to these events but don't take action. First, you need to know who your client is and who you are trying to reach. Only go to events where you feel the right quality of people will be.

Identify your Contact of Influence (COI) potential categories

We know people who may have valuable connections.

Go to as many quality events as you can

Get out there! If you stay home, you're not benefitting anyone.

Consider taking a networking buddy.

Take a friend with you and maybe set a goal together or have a little contest between you, such as who can collect the most connections or business cards. Have a friendly competition. Another benefit of going with someone else is that if I meet someone, I can say, "You know, there's a really cool person I want you to meet." Sometimes it's easier to talk about somebody other than yourself. And it's good to have a buddy so you do not feel alone – even in a room of 30-50-100 people.

Send an individual email to everyone

Send an email to or call everyone you meet. Don't assume they will contact you if you give them your business card. I think there is potential for everyone.

Suggest a follow-up phone call, coffee, or a video chat.

Follow up with them. Connect with them. You never know where the connection will lead.

Connect on LinkedIn

It's pretty basic; just do it! I typically initiate LinkedIn connections.

Follow the rabbit hole

This is key. What do I mean by "follow the rabbit hole"? You never know where it will go or who that new connection knows. The average person knows 300 people (or if you're a millennial, you probably know 1000 people). I belong to a BNI business group, but my best resource, believe it or not, is a guy named Freddie. He was a blue-collar guy, dropped an F-bomb every three seconds, and owned a construction company. He was not a client of mine, but he happened to be a builder in Greenwich,

Connecticut, and friends with many high-profile CEO and CFO multi-millionaires/billionaires. He was the best referral source I've ever had.

Follow up. Follow up. Follow up.

You never know who you can connect with. Follow up with a quick text or email saying, "How's it going?" Do this once every six months.

Social Media

The second leg of the stool is social media. The key is to learn how to leverage social media positively.

Create the brand you want people to know you for

Back in the day, if you wanted to make a personal brand about you, you'd have to buy a billboard or a TV spot for half-million dollars. There wasn't an easy way to do it. But today, we have social media. And on it, you are a brand! So, you must ensure the brand you are creating represents you. It's important! Be transparent and authentic to who and what you're about. Don't try to be someone you're not.

Have a well-thought-out profile representing your brand

I'm a big believer in using LinkedIn. I've spent a lot of time and resources ensuring my profile represents who and what I'm about. LinkedIn is a phenomenal tool that allows you to really represent who and what you're about. People will do business with people they know, like, and trust. LinkedIn is a great tool for that.

Consider a profile video of yourself

Have a little intro about yourself.

Continually add relevant connections

I am on LinkedIn almost every day. Take advantage of the "You may know" section to find connections. I often hear, "I don't want to connect with someone unless I really know them." Let me ask you this, What does LeBron James do that pays him the most? Basketball? No, he earns money as an influencer because he has over a million followers. How would you like to have more followers that want to know you? Why wouldn't you want to have followers that you have a presence for? You can communicate with them. It's phenomenal. LinkedIn doesn't have all the tools that an extensive CRM has, but it has the basics to get you started.

Your net worth is in direct proportion to your network

Your connections should be relevant to you. It's a cliché, but it's true: Your net worth is directly proportional to your network. Make your network big. When I first joined LinkedIn and was working for a different company, I had about 200 connections. But I've been continually building up my network.

Post frequently but be relevant

Put up some content. Videos are great. I started doing them and loved them! Be relevant. Not salesy, relevant.

Be active

It's important to like, comment, and reach out. LinkedIn has great tools (e.g., notifications of job changes, promotions, anniversaries, and birthdays). When people respond, I respond with a custom message, such as "Let's catch up with a phone call." Leverage it.

LinkedIn Exchange

LinkedIn Exchange allows you to connect one of your connections with someone else in a three-way conversation.

I have gotten business from LinkedIn because people read their LinkedIn messages.

Unconventional

The third leg of the stool is *unconventional,* and it involves meeting people everywhere and anywhere. Start conversations on purpose. My goal is to meet three strangers every day. I love doing it because I get to meet cool people and see how I can be of value.

The world is your networking event

You can meet people everywhere. You just need to be open. When I talk to people, I am amazed at how people react when I start a conversation with them.

Break the ice – "Where are you from, and what do you do?"

Say something – anything! Like, "Cool logo!" or "Nice glasses!" or if you see a logo from a college, "Hey, did you go there?" You don't need the perfect icebreaker. I've said some cool things that were met with a blank stare, and I've also said some stupid things that got a really good reaction. It's not about what you say to break the ice. You can start with "Where are you from?" or "What do you do?" Pretty straightforward. Those two topics can get into a lot of detail in a conversation.

Per "How to Win Friends and Influence People" by Dale Carnegie, a person's favorite topic is themselves. What is their favorite word? Their name. So, do a lot of that – talk about them. Don't talk about yourself.

Don't pitch to them. Find out about them. Believe they'll want to know about you eventually.

Open posture and smile; be warm and confident

Be friendly. Smile with your eyes. Don't have a goofy smile. Be warm.

Don't be afraid to make a fool of yourself

Don't worry about it. Trust that people won't be thinking about you later. They have their own problems.

Half the world is waiting for the other half to say hello

You will be amazed at how true that is when you talk to people.

It's like petting a dog

Talking to people is like petting a dog. You might get a fierce growl when you try to pet a Doberman Pincher. A Chihuahua yips at you. A Golden Retriever will lick you. People are like that. The problem is you don't know the breed, so you have to talk to find out. If you get a Doberman Pincher, just walk away. Dogs have three reactions, and so do people. Dogs' reactions are: (1) They want to lick you, be petted, and get really excited; (2) Growl and don't want to be bothered; (3) Don't care and walk away (like a cat). So don't worry about the reaction. It's not you; it's them.

Send a text or email and connect on LinkedIn

After I meet someone, I will send a text or an email to connect with them on LinkedIn. It's so important not to let that one contact be it. Connect again.

Be open

That's the biggest thing I want you to be thinking about – just be open. Be open for business, and be open to talk.

Follow-up call and/or coffee

Follow up to really stay in touch.

Here's my final thought: If I can do it, you can!

The Power of a Personal Message or Note

There is a benefit to using a personal touch.

First, let's talk "old school." Granted, we have texting, emailing, and all sorts of messaging through social media. Those are all great tools, but let's not forget the value of a handwritten note. Yes – a personal note, an actual card mailed to someone's home. Incredible value!

I remember networking with Rob Thomas, a great guy, and afterward, he sent me a personal note and a small gift. I wasn't expecting any of that, but it was great! The note was handwritten, thought out, and personalized and had real value. So if you know somebody you want to thank or encourage, send them a nice note.

Another type of effective messaging is a voice message. I don't mean leaving a voice message – I'm talking about sending one. When you send a long text message, it can be d to read, especially for those with learning disabilities. Avoid "scrollers"! Also, it's difficult to capture the emotions, feelings, and expressions in a text or message.

Sometimes internalize the written message, or we project onto it the mood we're in when we're reading it. Noise from something else when we read a message can cause us to interpret that written message as someone who is maybe annoyed with us – but they didn't mean it that way at all! Emojis and other images are a great way to convey your sentiment and help a little; there is nothing better than someone hearing your voice, tone, tempo, and volume.

A voice message allows you to differentiate, personalize, and let others feel your passion, energy, and warmth – whatever you want to convey. Voice messaging shouldn't completely replace text or written messages. Only use them when the message will be long, or you want to convey a certain feeling. Also, don't forget that "old school" handwritten notes; those work well too.

Do You Have an Intro Video?

Do you have an intro video? The importance of one is that it's personal – a person can see and hear you. It can help you connect with others because they can see and listen to you.

Consider hiring a videographer. I did, and he helped me create a 3-5 minute video. I feel it was worthwhile to do.

You can also use video if you're job-seeking. Send a custom video in an email to the hiring manager. It doesn't have to be long, maybe 30 seconds to say, "I'd love the opportunity to meet you," or something similar. If you're articulate, that's an asset for you. So why not leverage that asset?

Trusting somebody if you can see and hear them is much easier than reading a text or email. Many people prefer to hide behind the written text, but I believe that's not very effective if you really want to connect with people.

Create an intro video because people want to know more about you. I have had a lot of success connecting with others who have viewed my intro video. So, I feel there's great value in it, and well worth the effort.

Relationships are Not 50/50 – They are 100/0

We have been taught that relationships are a 50/50 deal, but I'm here to tell you that's wrong—in my humble but accurate opinion. I've learned that those who give unconditionally, who serve and do things without an agenda, are the ones who have incredible relationships.

In a 50/50 relationship, you're looking for something in return. When you do that, you're expecting the other person to change. Don't expect anything from someone else. Instead, be who you need to be.

I've learned to be the best person I can be, to serve and give. I believe if you do the right stuff, it eventually comes back to you.

Give the Gift of Connection and Reach Out

Many of us focus on giving others physical gifts – things, and there is nothing wrong with that. There is a lot to be said about generosity. One of my mentors told me, "The secret of living is giving." I want to put a different perspective on that – let the gift of giving be the gift of connection.

Many people are hurting because human connection is lacking. While it may be challenging to be with people physically, you can still connect in some way. Pick up the phone and call someone, or jump on a video call. Connect through social media. Reach out – connect with somebody!

Think about people in your life who you haven't connected with in a while or who could really use a connection. If you are into meditation or prayer, you could pray or meditate on it, and someone will come to mind that you could reach out to.

It's great to reach out to someone and connect with them. No with agenda – just connect and say hello. Ask, "What can I do to help you?" We are humans, and humans crave interaction. So let's be in giving mode with the gift of connection. Also, don't be "too busy" to connect with others or wear "busy" like a badge of honor. Now is the time to slow down, reflect, take a deep breath, and connect with people.

Conclusion

I hope and pray that by following the four pillars outlined in this book, you believe that you can be a master connector. This book details how to become others-focused, listen to others, and build relationships based on mutual trust and respect. By having the grit to overcome obstacles, you've learned to persevere through challenges and setbacks to achieve your goals.

By connecting authentically, you've seen that we can build genuine relationships based on honesty and integrity. And by building a community and growing our connections, we can create a network of like-minded individuals who can support us on our journey. I truly believe that anyone who follows the principles outlined in this book and is willing to put in the work can become a master connector.

As we close the book, let us remember that in our weakness, there is power. We all have unique strengths and weaknesses. However, embracing our weaknesses and insecurities allows us to lead with them and be vulnerable, creating powerful connections. We will also find that by releasing the power these strongholds have over us, we will become powerfully confident.

So let us continue striving for greatness and never forget the power of true human connection.

Gratefulness and Thankfulness

First and most importantly, I need to give the honor and glory to my Heavenly Father. Without Him I wouldn't be here or be the man I am today, and this book would certainly <u>not</u> be possible. All of the thanks goes to God! My faith-walk and spiritual journey is extremely meaningful and very important to me. However, it is personal experience to me and prefer to share it on a one-on-one basis, rather than in a mass-setting, like this book. If you would like to know more about my journey and beliefs, please reach out to me and I will share it all with you.

From an earthly perspective, I couldn't have written this book without the ongoing support of my amazing wife, the continued guidance of the mentors in my life, the constant encouragement and support of my ghost-writer Val Roskens Tews. Big thanks also goes to my Master Connector Show co-host, Cameron Toth, for always pushing me to be a better version of me. And a special thank you to the entrepreneurs and leaders who contributed to this book.

There have been so many others, too many to name, from my biological family to my adopted family (my community and network), my martial arts family, my partners/affiliates, and my friends. The phrase "It takes a village" really applies here!

Contact Steve Spiro

To reach Steve Spiro, go to www.stevespiro.com or https://sspiro.com

To hire Steve Spiro as a speaker, go to www.soiro-global.com

To Learn more about the Master Connector Show, go to www.MasterConnector.Show

Or scan the QR code below

Made in the USA
Middletown, DE
12 June 2023

32168384R00099